HISTORIES
OF LEGAL
LITERATURE

Burkhard Gotthelf Struve, *Bibliotheca iuris selecta* (Jena: E. C. Bailliar, 1703). Rare Book Collection, Lillian Goldman Law Library, Yale Law School; reproduced with permission.

HISTORIES
OF LEGAL
LITERATURE

A Hundred Years of
English-Language Scholarship

MICHAEL WIDENER &
RYAN GREENWOOD

TALBOT
PUBLISHING
Clark, New Jersey
2024

© 2024 Michael Widener and Ryan Greenwood.

ISBN: 978-1-61619-691-2

TALBOT PUBLISHING

AN IMPRINT OF
The Lawbook Exchange, Ltd.
33 Terminal Avenue
Clark, New Jersey 07066-1321

Please see our website for a selection of our other publications and fine facsimile reprints of classic works of legal history www.lawbookexchange.com

Library of Congress Cataloging-in-Publication Data

Names: Widener, Michael, author. I Greenwood, Ryan, author.
Title: Histories of legal literature : a hundred years of English-language scholarship / Michael Widener & Ryan Greenwood.
Description: First edition. I Clark : Talbot Publishing, an Imprint of The Lawbook Exchange, Ltd., 2024. I Includes bibliographical references and index. I Summary: "A comprehensive bibliography of historical studies of legal literature published in English from 1921 to 2022"-- Provided by publisher.
Identifiers: LCCN 2024030376 I ISBN 9781616196912 (hardcover)
Subjects: LCSH: Law--History--Bibliographies. I English philology--Study and teaching--History.
Classification: LCC K140 .W53 2024 I DDC 016.34--dc23/eng/20240712
LC record available at https://lccn.loc.gov/2024030376

Printed in the United States of America on acid-free paper

CONTENTS

About the Frontispiece

The image is taken from the first edition of Burkhard Gotthelf Struve's *Bibliotheca iuris selecta* (Jena, 1703), a popular legal bibliography that went through nine editions in the 18th century. Burkhard Gotthelf Struve (1671-1738) came from a family of distinguished German jurists and was known as a historian as well as a legal scholar. The illustration shows a law library with signs designating the major branches of legal literature: the upper level contains (l-r) public law, feudal law, and civil law, and the lower level has manuscript codices, canon law, and criminal law. At the lower left is a pile of ancient coins and broken monuments topped by a Latin inscription, "Nova fuere" ("All was once new"), which is a quotation from Tacitus ("All things, which we consider now as most ancient, were once new").

Acknowledgments

In the decade that has passed since we initiated this project, we have accumulated many debts. Our greatest debt is to Alison Burke and Craig Kirkland of the Lillian Goldman Law Library, Yale Law School, and David Zopfi-Jordan of the University of Minnesota Law Library, who cheerfully and efficiently honored dozens and dozens of requests for downloads and interlibrary loans.

We are also indebted to our cadre of thoughtful readers – Jonathan Bush, Ross Davies, Scott Dewey, Joel Fishman, Michael Hannon, Nicholas Mignanelli, Agustín Parise, Fred Shapiro, Otto Vervaart, Michael von der Linn, and Emma Molina Widener – for their feedback on our final draft.

Thanks for favors large and small to KB Beck, Otto Danwerth, Laurel Davis, Bruno Debaenst, Lionel Epstein, John D. Gordan III, Kathryn James, Randall Lesaffer, Georges Martyn, Douglas J. Osler, Pedro Rueda Ramírez, Larissa Reid, Mark Somos, John C. Wei, Henry Granville Widener, and Anders Winroth.

We owe a special thanks to Gregory Talbot, president of Talbot Publishing and Lawbook Exchange, for his advice and support, and to Peter Lo Ricco, Talbot Publishing's graphic designer.

> *"Any serious history of law must also be a history of law books."*
>
> – Michael H. Hoeflich[1]

Introduction

As William Faulkner famously wrote, "The past is never dead. It's not even past." Law is intrinsically backward-looking, built on judicial precedents, legislation, rules, commentaries, even customs identified with normative traditions and accepted reasoning. Although the history of the law, in its widest scope, is not often pursued by practicing lawyers, it catches in its net every aspect of modern legal theory and practice. Legal history has found a sturdy place in U.S. law schools and has been applied widely, beyond its own academic sphere, to contextualize social, political, and economic history, as well as histories of art and culture. Legal history is today, more than ever, an indispensable lens through which to view many kinds of historical development.

The history of the law is known above all through its literature, an extraordinarily diverse body of texts. For both legal historians and law librarians, an understanding of how this literature evolved and was transmitted is essential. Cultural historians cannot overlook the role of legal literature in the broader history of books and reading practices. In addition, the historical development of law libraries, the profession of law librarianship, and the tools of the profession are inextricably bound with the history of the literatures they preserve. Particularly for those librarians, like ourselves, who

---

[1] "Legal History and the History of the Book: Variations on a Theme," *University of Kansas Law Review* 46 (1998): 415-431, at 416; no. 432 in the checklist.

collect and manage historical collections of legal literature, there is a pressing need to refer to historical studies of legal literature, to better understand and build these collections.

Accordingly, this checklist began with our own efforts to understand the historical law collections in our care, to nurture these collections, and to promote their use for teaching and research in the academic law libraries where we have worked. We turned, naturally, to legal history, but especially to those studies and bibliographies that focused on the history of legal literature.

Beginning in 2010, we developed reading lists on the history of legal literature for the students of a week-long intensive course in the University of Virginia's Rare Book School, "Law Books: History and Connoisseurship."[2] Through our common work as law librarians and through our teaching, both of us became convinced that the history of legal literature has a broad constituency: special collections librarians, legal historians, book historians, book dealers, collectors, and legal research librarians. In 2013, we began assembling a comprehensive bibliography of historical studies of legal literature published in English. The result is the checklist of 998 numbered items that follows.

The checklist, we hope, will serve several purposes beyond simply providing access to English-language scholarship on legal literature in the past one hundred years. It is meant to stimulate research in general, based on the rich scholarly resources that have been produced (many of them, incidentally, by law librarians). It also aims to show by comparison, partly through its index and accompanying statistics, the strengths and gaps in scholarship on the history of legal literature, and thus to suggest opportunities for new contributions. Librarians and researchers may benefit from the checklist, but also book dealers, private collectors, and even legal practitioners,

[2] The course is the successor to "Collecting the History of Anglo-American Law," which Morris L. Cohen and David Warrington taught from 1989 to 2006. Widener began teaching the course in 2010; Greenwood joined as co-instructor for the 2018 and 2021 classes.

who seek an overview of types of literature, their periods of publication, and the experts who have studied them extensively. Further, we hope the list encourages comparative studies of the literatures of different jurisdictions around the world, to enrich our understanding of laws and traditions that have intersected and whose literatures have shared, to some extent, functions and forms.

Finally, we can note here, and discuss further below, that the checklist takes an expansive approach to the literature of the law, in the hope that new historical connections will be identified and studied.

In the following text and footnotes, references to the numbered items in the checklist will be by item number, directing the reader to the checklist for the full bibliographic citation. Thus, for example, Douglas Lind's "An Economic Analysis of Early Casebook Publishing," *Law Library Journal* 96, no. 1 (Winter 2004): 95-126, will be referenced as "no. 560"; or "the works of Morris L. Cohen (nos. 192-205 and 661)."

A few words are in order regarding our choice of the term "checklist" instead of "bibliography" for our compilation of citations. *ABC for Book Collectors*,[3] a standard glossary for bibliographers, book collectors, and the book trade, recognizes two meanings for "bibliography": "One (the more familiar to the general public) is a reading list, a guide for further study or a list of works which have been consulted by the author ... The other, familiar to collectors, is the study of books as physical objects." The study of law books as physical objects has featured prominently in recent scholarship, and is reflected in our subject indexing. For clarity's sake, and in deference to the outstanding bibliographers who feature so prominently in our compilation – such as Morris Cohen, Ann Laeuchli, and Douglas Osler – we have opted for "checklist" as more appropriate for our "guide for further study."

[3] Nicolas Barker & Simran Thadani, *John Carter's ABC for Book Collectors* (9th ed.; New Castle, DE: Oak Knoll Press, 2016).

Scope of the Checklist

L egal scholarship, including legal history, and the library collections that support it are becoming increasingly globalized and diverse. That breadth is reflected in the checklist that follows, which brings together 998 historical studies of legal literature published in English during the last hundred years in 183 monographs, 275 essays in collective works, and 540 journal articles.[4] A passage from W. N. Osborough's "In Praise of Law Books" neatly summarizes the checklist's scope:

> The concern here is with law books down the centuries in all their ramifications and studied in conjunction with all their associations: why they came to be written, who wrote them, how they were produced, how they were circulated, the uses to which they were applied, the arrangements to secure their preservation.[5]

We define "legal literature" as the texts *of* the law shared by the participants in a legal system (statutes, constitutions, case reports, treatises, practice guides, student textbooks)[6] and works *about* the law aimed at more general audiences (law reform, popular works, juvenile literature), disseminated in a variety of formats, both tangible (printed books, manuscripts, periodicals, pamphlets, broadsides) and intangible (digital media, oral texts). This broad conception of legal literature seeks to promote new avenues for scholarship, teaching,

---

[4] We include five review essays among the articles (nos. 46, 47, 132, 708, and 962) that make significant contributions to the history of legal literature.

[5] No. 677, at 340.

[6] Law librarians would categorize sources such as statutes, constitutions, and case reports as primary sources, with treatises, textbooks, practice guides and law journals as secondary sources.

6

collection development, and cross-fertilization with other fields, especially the lively discipline of book history. "Legal literature" does not include archival records, printed or otherwise, such as court documents, personal notebooks, appellate briefs, or transactional legal documents.[7]

The checklist also takes a broad view of "historical studies." These include, for example, works that treat the publication and dissemination of legal literature, since these are integral both to book history and legal history; exhibition catalogs; histories and catalogs of particular libraries that shed light on how literature is collected and deemed important by a given individual or period; and even noted auction catalogs, that document historic law collections and their sales. The history of legal literature is blessed with a number of superb bibliographies, themselves works of deep historical scholarship, which together with library catalogs and auction catalogs supply a large corpus of historical data on legal literature. Citations of research guides are limited to those that devote substantial attention to the history of legal literature.[8]

As the checklist demonstrates, histories of Anglo-American legal literature are plentiful. The challenge for English-speaking researchers and librarians (a challenge we faced early in our careers) is finding English-language histories of legal literatures from outside of the common law world. We made a concerted effort to seek out such works for inclusion in the checklist. The common law has never been as insular as some of its champions have portrayed it; borrowings from civil law systems have been going on for centuries. French and

---

[7] We made an exception for studies of commonplace books (see no. 435), since they document the dissemination of legal literature and served as models for the early printed abridgments of English common law.

[8] See nos. 101, 271, 395, 397, 520, 661, 741, 806, and 807. Between 1912 and 1976 the Law Library of Congress published guides to the legal literatures of Germany, Spain, France, and many Latin American nations that include useful historical overviews, such as *Guide to the Law and Legal Literature of Spain* (Washington, DC: G.P.O., 1915) and *Revised Guide to the Law & Legal Literature of Mexico* (Washington, DC: Law Library of Congress, 1973), which are not included in the checklist.

Hispanic law have profoundly shaped the law of Louisiana and the American Southwest. The fields of international and comparative law, and the growing number of LL.M. programs and joint programs between U.S. law schools and their foreign counterparts, also require an understanding of the historical literatures of legal systems worldwide. Indeed, Laura Beck Varela writes that, "As a field of knowledge, the history of law could even be defined as a long history of interconnectedness between actors of different (sometimes even remote) spaces and times."[9]

In restricting the checklist to English-language works, we must acknowledge the enormous body of publications in other languages. Among these are many of the essential reference works on the history of legal literature, such as Ter Meulen & Diermanse's bibliograpy of Hugo Grotius[10] or Helmut Coing's monumental *Handbuch der Quellen und Literatur der neueren europäischen Privatrechtsgeschichte.*[11] Diligent readers will find citations to many foreign-language histories of legal literature in the footnotes of works in the checklist. Several of the authors cited in the checklist have published many of their studies of legal literature in other languages, including Laura Beck-Varela, Gero Dolezalek, Robert Feenstra, Domenico Maffei, Agustín Parise, Maria Alessandra Panzanelli Fratoni, Frank Sotermeer, and Alain Wijffels. English translations of some of these studies would be welcome.

The checklist covers the past century of historical scholarship on legal literature, beginning in 1921. A century is a common time frame for retrospectives, but in the case of our checklist it is more than a cliché. It was in 1921 that Frederick Hicks published *Men and Books Famous in the Law* (no.

---

[9]   No. 59, at 195.

[10]   Jacob ter Meulen & P. J. J. Diermanse, *Bibliographie des écrits imprimés de Hugo Grotius* (La Haye: M. Nijhoff, 1950).

[11]   *Handbuch der Quellen und Literatur der neueren europäischen Privatrechtsgeschichte* (Helmut Coing, ed.; 3 vols.; München: C. H. Beck, 1973-1988).

422), a work that remains one of the classics in the field. That same decade saw the appearance of several other classics: Joseph Beale's *Bibliography of Early English Law Books* (no. 58), Bertha Putnam's *Early Treatises on the Practice of the Justices of the Peace* (no. 757), and Percy Winfield's *Chief Sources of English Legal History* (no. 976). On the other hand, very few titles before 1921 remain useful today. One could mention *The Charlemagne Tower Collection of American Colonial Laws*,[12] still a standard reference source; Van Vechten Veeder's "The English Reports, 1292-1865";[13] and a personal favorite of ours, *Lawyers' Merriments* by David Murray,[14] a delightful romp through the oddities of legal literature. Further back in time, John William Wallace's *The Reporters, Chronologically Arranged*[15] and J. G. Marvin's *Legal Bibliography*,[16] while dated, continue to be informative and often-cited reference sources.

There is a great deal of valuable research and discussion of legal literature that could not be included in an already large checklist. With four exceptions,[17] we have avoided citing

[12]   Philadelphia: J. B. Lippincott Co., 1890; reprinted Littleton, CO: F. B. Rothman, 1990.

[13]   *Harvard Law Review* 15, no. 1 (May 1901): 1-25.

[14]   Glasgow: J. MacLehose, 1912; reprinted Clark, NJ: Lawbook Exchange, 2005.

[15]   John William Wallace, *The Reporters, Chronologically Arranged* (1st ed.: Philadelphia: I. R. Bailey, 1844; 4th ed.: Boston: Soule & Bugbee, 1882, reprinted Buffalo, NY: W. S. Hein, 1995).

[16]   J. G. Marvin, *Legal Bibliography, A Thesaurus of American, English, Irish, and Scotch law: Together with Some Continental Treatises* (Philadelphia: T. & J.W. Johnson, 1847).

[17]   The chapter on "Legal Literature" in John H. Baker's *Introduction to English Legal History* (no. 41) is to date the best compact overview of the whole of English legal literature. In "The Torch is Passed: In-Chambers Opinions and the Reporter of Decisions in Historical Perspective" (no. 506), Craig Joyce gives a succinct account of U.S. Supreme Court reporters from the court's inception to the 21st century. Julia Rudolph's chapter on "Law Books, Legal Knowledge" in her *Common Law and Enlightenment in England, 1689-1750* (no. 804) resurrects the extensive legal literature of an era "denigrated or dismissed by

chapters from general histories.[18] We have excluded general biographies of legal authors (William Blackstone and Edward Coke, for example), in favor of biographical treatments that focus on an author's literary output. Legislative history, and histories of legal education, the legal profession, legal doctrine, and codification are other fields in which legal literature figures prominently, but are outside the scope of the checklist. However, the reader will find many citations to such works in the items that are included.[19]

One particularly notable exclusion is critical editions of legal texts, chief among these the Annual Volumes of the Selden Society (now at 135 volumes and counting).[20] Some of the

---

modern scholars" (at 31). "Ten Greatest Law Books" from Bernard Schwartz's *Book of Legal Lists: The Best and Worst in American Law* (no. 820) is a leading legal historian's take on ten books that "changed the very way Americans think about law and the manner in which courts operate."

[18] General histories with useful reviews of legal literature include Lawrence M. Friedman, *A History of American Law* (4th ed.; New York: Oxford University Press, 2019); William S. Holdsworth, *A History of English Law* (17 vols.; London: Sweet & Maxwell, 1972-1992); John H. Langbein, Renée Lettow Lerner, & Bruce P. Smith, *History of the Common Law: The Development of Anglo-American Legal Institutions* (New York: Aspen Publishers, 2009); Alan Watson, *Legal Transplants: An Approach to Comparative Law* (2nd ed.; Athens, GA: University of Georgia Press, 1993); Manlio Bellomo, *The Common Legal Past of Europe: 1000-1800* (Washington, DC: Catholic University of America Press, 1995); Antonio Padoa-Schioppa, *A History of Law in Europe: From the Early Middle Ages to the Twentieth Century* (Cambridge, UK: Cambridge University Press, 2017); Bart Wauters & Marco de Benito, *The History of Law in Europe: An Introduction* (Cheltenham, UK: Edgar Elgar Publishing, 2017); and *The Cambridge History of Medieval Canon Law* (Anders Winroth & John C. Wei, eds.; Cambridge, UK: Cambridge University Press, 2022).

[19] The long-running debate on the French and Spanish sources of the Louisiana Civil Code illustrates our method of selection. Many of the works indexed under "American law – Louisiana" in the checklist relate to the debate. We chose them because they focused on the role of law books in the code's genesis. One of the debate's leading protagonists, Warren Billings, summarizes the "overwhelming accumulation of literature" on the debate in "James Morgan Bradford and Print Culture in Early Louisiana" (no. 92), at 5, citing many works that we excluded. For a broad overview of the codification movement in the 18th and 19th centuries, international in scope, see Agustín Parise, "The Place of the Louisiana Civil Code in the Hispanic Civil Codifications," no. 707.

[20] For a complete listing, see https://www.seldensociety.ac.uk/publications/

most valuable studies of English legal literature can be found in the often-cited introductions to these volumes, especially on the history of English case reporting. By the same token, we excluded reprint editions of important legal works, such as the Legal Classics Library published by Gryphon Editions[21] and the Lawbook Exchange Reprints series,[22] which include useful introductions and notes by leading legal historians. Including all these works would have added several hundred entries to the checklist.

As regards the publishing history of American law, a large body of work by Robert D. Armstrong deserves mention, which appeared in *Papers of the Bibliographical Society of America* over the course of two decades. Since Armstrong's articles focus on pre-statehood public printing in the American West, they did not fit the scope of the checklist, but they contain valuable information on the publication history of territorial statutes and case reports.[23]

---

annual-volumes/.

[21] See https://gryphoneditions.com/.

[22] See https://www.lawbookexchange.com/publishing.php.

[23] See: "Nevada's Public Printing, Chiefly in 1869: Additional Notes to Armstrong, 'Nevada Printing History,'" *Papers of the Bibliographical Society of America* (hereinafter *PBSA*) 81, no. 4 (Dec. 1987): 465-478; "'Printed in Maine': Montana's Down East Printing." *PBSA* 84, no. 2 (June 1990): 158-167; "Idaho Territory's San Francisco Printers, 1864-1866," *PBSA* 85, no. 1 (March 1991): 49-65; "'The Work Must Be Performed Elsewhere': The Printing of Montana's Laws and Legislative Journals, 1866-1881," *PBSA* 88, no. 4 (Dec. 1994): 437-499; "'A Proper Business Prudence': Arizona's Extraterritorial Printing, 1865-1887, and an 1889 Variation," *PBSA* 90, no. 2 (June 1996): 195-215, and 90, no. 3 (Sept. 1996): 343-366; "'Good Square Men in Their Dealings': Wyoming Territory's Imported Public Printers," *PBSA* 91, no. 3 (Sept. 1997): 409-422; "'Clothed with the Authority': A Dispute over Public Printing in Colorado Territory," *PBSA* 93, no. 3 (Sept. 1999): 359-377; "'Favoritism Has Been Practiced': New Capital, Old Printer in Dakota Territory," *PBSA* 94, no. 2 (June 2000): 235-254; "'The Only Alternative Course': Incidents in Nevada Printing History," *PBSA* 95, no. 1 (Mar. 2001): 97-115; "'The Work Should Be Done with Economy': Montana's Law and Legislative Journal Printing, 1883-89," *PBSA* 98, no. 2 (June 2004): 163-190; "'Impenetrable Obscurity': The Comptroller, the Secretary, and Territorial Printing," *PBSA* 99, no. 3 (Sept. 2005): 411-425; "'I Scornfully Rejected the Terms': Wyoming Territory's Public Printing, 1870-

Within the confines of our scope, we have endeavored to be comprehensive. In spite of our efforts, there are undoubtedly sins of commission and omission in the finished product. We will be grateful for suggestions from our readers.

74," *PBSA* 101, no. 1 (Mar. 2007): 73-89; and "'We Have Seen Many a Worse Job Done "Further East"': Dakota's Public Printing, 1862-3," *PBSA* 101, no. 2 (June 2007): 149-165.

Arrangement of the Checklist

T he entries in the checklist are sorted first by author, then by date (earliest to latest), and finally, for works by an author published in a single year, by genre (monographs first, then book chapters, and finally articles). Items with multiple authors are sorted according to the first author named in the publication; co-authors are ignored in sorting an author's works. An index of co-authors follows the checklist.

The author arrangement serves to highlight those authors who have contributed most to the history of legal literature. For authors who are the acknowledged leaders in their respective fields (such as John H. Baker in English legal literature, Morris L. Cohen in American legal literature, or Joel Fishman in Pennsylvania legal literature), the author arrangement provides mini-bibliographies for those fields.

For most authors, the form of the author's name is the one given in the publication. When the author's name appears in various forms, the name is standardized; thus "Baker, John H." is used instead of "Baker, J. H.", etc. Authors' names are repeated with each entry, for ease of reference.

Entries include URLs only for articles in open-access, online-only journals (for example, no. 80). However, a number of monographic exhibition catalogs published over the last several years are more readily available in open-access scholarship repositories than in their original print formats.[24]

---

[24] For the exhibition catalogs published by the Boston College Law Library (nos. 62-64, 82, 255-262, 264-265), search the titles at https://lira.bc.edu/. The Yale Law Library exhibition catalogs (nos. 15, 599, 747, 943, 976) can be searched at https://openyls.law.yale.edu/. The Kenneth Spencer Research Library's excellent *Civil, Canon and Common: Aspects of Legal History* (no. 529) can be downloaded at http://hdl.handle.net/1808/11766.

14

We made an effort to note reprints, but some have probably escaped our notice.

In most cases, relevant chapters in collective works are listed separately to enable better access. The exceptions are seven titles, encyclopedic in scope, whose entire contents are both relevant and internally uniform. Listing the individual chapters would have significantly increased the size of the checklist without a corresponding improvement in access. These are *The Cambridge History of Medieval Canon Law* (no. 168) *The Formation and Transmission of Western Legal Culture: 150 Books That Made the Law in the Age of Printing* (no. 347), *An Introductory Survey of the Sources and Literature of Scots Laws* (no. 482), *Law and the Christian Tradition in Italy: The Legacy of the Great Jurists* (no. 553), *Pre-Statehood Legal Materials: A Fifty-state Research Guide* (no. 741), *Stair Tercentenary Studies* (no. 860), and *Virginia Law Books: Essays and Bibliographies* (no. 924). These seven collective works are entered in the checklist by title, not by their editors' last names.

The bibliographic citation style used for the checklist is generally the one set out in the *Chicago Manual of Style*, 17th edition, with a few modifications. Repeated names of authors are not replaced with long dashes, so that each entry is self-sufficient and can be copied without referring to a preceding entry for the omitted name. In entries for contributions to multi-author books, names of editors follow the book's title and are enclosed in parentheses along with the imprint, with the page range at the end (see no. 6 for an example), resulting in citations that are tighter and that more closely parallel the citations for articles. All page ranges are given in full, thus "143-178" instead of "143-78." Names of multiple authors or editors are connected with the ampersand in place of "and."

Histories of Legal Literature, 1921-2022: An Overview

The checklist and its index are more than handy reference tools. They also serve as a dataset, a bibliometric if you please, outlining the contours and trajectory of the field. Following are some general observations. We will be happy to provide raw data to others who wish to venture further.

First, let's recap the numbers. The checklist consists of 998 publications: 540 journal articles, 275 essays in collective works, and 183 monographs. They represent the work of 611 individual authors (including co-authors) and 10 corporate authors.

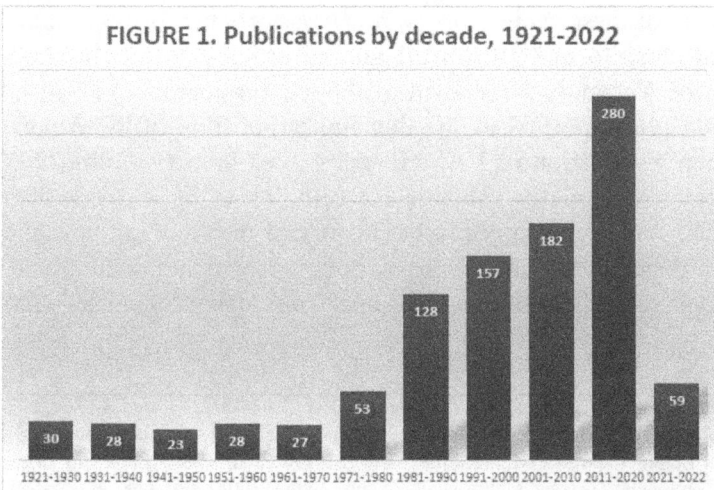

FIGURE 1. Publications by decade, 1921-2022

For the first half of the century, 1921-1970, the checklist logs 136 publications (an average of 27 per decade), accounting for only 14 percent of all the publications in the checklist. As shown in Figure 1, the number of historical studies of legal literature began to skyrocket in the 1980s. The

16

second decade of the 21st century alone accounts for a quarter of all publications.

Several factors can account for this growth. The number of scholarly journals in history, the humanities, and law has grown exponentially during the past century.[25] The first English-language journal devoted to legal history, the *American Journal of Legal History*, appeared in 1957, followed by the *Journal of Legal History* in the United Kingdom (1980), *Law and History Review* in the United States (1983), and *Fundamina: A Journal of Legal History* in South Africa (1992). In recent decades, English has been an increasingly common language in the multilingual legal history journals of continental Europe, such as the venerable Dutch journal *Tijdschrift voor Rechtsgeschiedenis / The Legal History Review*,[26] and *Rechtsgeschichte - Legal History (Rg)*,[27] the journal of the Max Planck Institute for Legal History and Legal Theory.

The 540 journal articles come from 188 different journals. One of these, *Law Library Journal*, accounts for 95 articles, or close to one-fifth of all journal articles in the checklist. (See Appendix 1 for a list of the leading journals.) From its inception in 1908 as the flagship publication of the American Association of Law Libraries, *Law Library Journal* has been particularly valuable for bringing to light overlooked and forgotten sources in the history of the common law, and in documenting law libraries, both personal and institutional. The second leading serial, *American Journal of Legal His-*

---

[25] For the growth in U.S. law reviews, see Michael L. Closen & Robert J. Dzielak, "The History and Influence of the Law Review Institution" (no. 188), at 15; and Lawrence M. Friedman, "Law Reviews and Legal Scholarship: Some Comments," *Denver Law Review* 75, no. 2 (Jan. 1998): 661-668, at 662-663. For U.K. and Australian law journals, see Ilija Vickovich, "Law Journals: From Discourse to Pedagogy," *Legal Education Review* 25, no. 1 (2015): 65-94, at 71-75. For the growth in academic journals generally, see Michael Mabe, "The Growth and Number of Serials," *Serials* 16, no. 2 (July 2003): 191-197.

[26] https://brill.com/view/journals/lega/lega-overview.xml?language=en.

[27] https://www.lhlt.mpg.de/publications/journals.

tory, represented by 22 articles, has highlighted works on nineteenth-century American legal literature. *Legal Reference Services Quarterly*, in third place, is sometimes less acknowledged in its role as a publisher of historical studies, yet it has published some significant contributions in this area. In fourth place with sixteen articles each are the *Journal of Legal History*, from Great Britain, and *Grotiana*, a journal dedicated to the life and influence of Hugo Grotius.[28] In fifth place is another pair of noteworthy journals. While some of the twelve articles from *Irish Jurist* deal with Irish legal literature, several represent important contributions to the history of English and American legal literature by such prominent historians as John Baker, Paul Brand, Morris Cohen, and David Ibbetson. *Unbound*, the journal of the Legal History & Rare Book Special Interest Section of the American Association of Law Libraries, is noteworthy as the only journal dedicated to the history of legal literature, and also as being open-access.[29]

One quarter of the checklist consists of 275 chapters from 146 collective works. A mere dozen of these works account for a third of all chapters and close to one-tenth of the checklist as a whole. Another seven collective works, encyclopedic in nature, are entered as monographs, as explained previously.[30]

---

[28] *Grotiana*'s high ranking is due to a recent series of ten reports produced by the Grotius Census Bibliography, a project sponsored by the Max Planck Institute for Comparative Public Law and International Law (nos. 220-228 and 857) to produce a worldwide census of surviving copies of the first ten editions of the international law classic by Hugo Grotius, *De iure belli ac pacis*. Careful readers will note that the final three reports on the census, nos. 226-228, were published in 2023. We judged it preferable to include these instead of amputating the series at our checklist's cutoff date of 2022. The project's final report, scheduled for publication in 2025, promises to be a landmark in bibliography and book history.

[29] https://www.aallnet.org/lhrbsis/resources-publications/unbound/.

[30] Again, these are *The Cambridge History of Medieval Canon Law* (no. 168), *The Formation and Transmission of Western Legal Culture: 150 Books That Made the Law in the Age of Printing* (no. 347), *An Introductory Survey of the Sources and Literature of Scots Laws* (no. 482), *Law and the Christian Tradition in Italy: The Legacy of the Great Jurists* (no. 553), *Pre-Statehood Legal Materials: A Fifty-state Research Guide* (no. 741), *Stair Tercentenary Studies*

One could build a substantial collection on the history of legal literature from these nineteen volumes alone. They are listed in Appendix 2.

As mentioned earlier, the checklist's author arrangement highlights the contributions of individual authors. Appendix 3 lists the leading authors (those with five or more publications). All of them are recommended reading, but we single out the top five.

Michael H. Hoeflich belongs at the top of the list not only for the sheer number of publications he has authored (30 in our checklist, spanning four decades), but also for the breadth of their subjects, ranging from the late Roman Empire (no. 428) to late 19th-century Kansas (no. 624). Hoeflich is an evangelist for incorporating book history into legal history (see no. 432), and he practices what he preaches. The epigraph by Hoeflich which opens the present study reflects the inspiration we drew from his approach. He has focused primarily on how all sorts of legal texts – from the ephemeral to the canonical, from foreign to native – were printed, published, sold, and shared in 19th-century America.

Sir John H. Baker is the leading scholar of the history of English law. From his prolific body of work on English law, we have selected 23 publications that exhibit his deep engagement with the historical literature of English common law in printed books and manuscripts. His contributions to *The Cambridge History of the Book in Britain* (nos. 30-31) and the chapter on legal literature in his *Introduction to English Legal History* (no. 41) are essential starting points. Unfortunately, some of Baker's oft-cited contributions to the field, in the introductions to the fourteen Annual Volumes of the Selden Society he has edited, lie outside the scope of the checklist.[31]

(no. 860), and *Virginia Law Books: Essays and Bibliographies* (no. 924). Citing their individual components would have added well over two hundred citations to the checklist without a corresponding improvement in access.

[31] See https://www.seldensociety.ac.uk/publications/annual-volumes/.

Douglas J. Osler, third on the list, is the leading bibliographer of the vast early modern literature of the European *ius commune*. In terms of sheer number of pages, he could very well be first on the list. His twenty publications in the checklist include six substantial bibliographies in nine volumes (nos. 318, 689, 690, 692, 695, and 696). Osler is not merely a practitioner of legal bibliography; he is a leading theorist and critic of modern bibliographic practice as regards early printed law books (see nos. 681-683 and 688). He has also published a number of articles on Roman-Dutch law (nos. 687 and 694), Justinian's Digest (no. 680), and legal humanism (nos. 691 and 697).

Following Osler in the list is the leading bibliographer of early American law, the late, great Morris L. Cohen, one of the most distinguished law librarians of the twentieth century. His six-volume *Bibliography of Early American Law* (no. 200), commonly referred to as BEAL, was the product of 35 years of research. It exhaustively records the monographic and trial literature of American law prior to 1860 with over 14,000 annotated entries and two fat volumes of indexes. He published much beyond this. His fifteen entries on the checklist range from work on lawyers' libraries (no. 192) to colonial American legal literature (no. 195), early U.S. Supreme Court reports (nos. 193 and 199, both with Sharon Hamby O'Connor), and legal lexicography (no. 203).

Rounding out the top five is Alain A. Wijffels. His writings on the legal literature of early modern Europe have been prolific, insightful, and useful. He is particularly attuned to the role of books in transmitting legal knowledge. Along with Douglas Osler (with whom he has carried on a lively debate),[32] he has provided road maps to the legal literature of Europe in the 16th and 17th centuries. His fifteen publications in the checklist don't fully reflect his contribution to the history of legal literature. He also edited two of the most important collections of essays on the subject: *Learning the Law:*

---

[32] See Osler's introductory essay in *Jurisprudence of the Baroque* (no. 695) and Wijffels' review (no. 962), especially the two lengthy footnotes at the end.

Teaching and the Transmission of Law in England, 1150-1900 (with Jonathan Bush) and *Case Law in the Making: The Techniques and Methods of Judicial Records and Law Reports* (see Appendix 2).

Histories of Legal Literature, 1921-2022: Contours of the English-Language Scholarship

T he checklist's index does more than simply guide the reader to publications on a particular topic. A scan of the index quickly reveals that some subject headings ("English law – Case reports" or "Libraries, private – United States") reference a few dozen publications, while others ("Brazilian law" or "Wheaton, Henry (1785-1848") reference only one. In essence, the index serves as a bibliometric, a measuring stick indicating which topics have received the most, or least, attention during the last century.

The subject headings fall into seven broad categories. The "Notes to the Index" section, below, describes them in detail. Briefly, they are: *bodies of law* (for example, Dutch law, Asian law, Roman law, international law), *legal genres* (case reports, treatises, etc.), *legal topics* (such as criminal law, domestic relations), *bibliographic genres* (bibliographies, catalogs, works on non-legal genres such as comics), *bibliographic topics* (publishing, indexing, illustration, and much more), *names* (of authors, publishers, etc.), and *chronological periods* (ancient and medieval). These categories provide a framework for describing the strengths and gaps in the past century of English-language scholarship on the history of legal literature.

Bodies of law

In a bibliography of English-language scholarship, it will come as no surprise that works on English and American legal literature dominate. The first priority and inclination of historians, lawyers, and librarians in the English-speaking world is naturally to understand their own legal literature.

Two-thirds of the entries that address bodies of law (592 of 881) are for works dealing with the legal literature of the British Isles, the British Commonwealth, and the United States. Among these are several useful overviews.[33]

Regarding the legal literature of individual U.S. states, three-fourths of the 88 publications address only four states: Louisiana (27), Virginia, (19), Pennsylvania (10), and Texas (9). For 34 states, nothing at all has been published on their legal literatures. Surely this is not for lack of interesting material. The article by Robert Mead and Michael Hoeflich on Kansas law books demonstrates some of the possibilities.[34]

The legal literatures of Virginia and Pennsylvania have benefited from the sustained attention of three individual historians over the course of their respective careers. In the case of Virginia, Warren M. Billings (who has also published on Louisiana law books) and W. Hamilton Bryson have written extensively and also edited collective works.[35] Over the course of two decades, Joel Fishman has singlehandedly written the history of Pennsylvania's legal literature in a dozen articles.

Louisiana's legal literature is by far the most studied of any U.S. state. The state's mixed system of civil and common law has served as a magnet for comparative legal historians

[33] George S. Grossman's *Legal Research: Historical Foundations of the Electronic Age* (no. 395) remains the most thorough overview of Anglo-American legal literature as a whole. The chapter on "Legal Literature" in John H. Baker's *An Introduction to English Legal History* (no. 41), and the chapters by Baker and Wilfrid Prest in *The Cambridge History of the Book in Britain* (nos. 30, 31, and 743) provide authoritative guides to the literature of English law, while *The Invention of Legal Research* by Joseph L. Gerken (no. 366), *The Yale Law School Guide to Research in American Legal History* by John B. Nann and Morris L. Cohen (no. 661), and *A History of American Law Publishing* by Erwin C. Surrency (no. 890) do the same for American legal literature.

[34] "Lawyers and Law Books in Nineteenth-Century Kansas" (no. 624).

[35] Billings was co-editor for *"Esteemed bookes of lawe" and the Legal Culture of Early Virginia* (see nos. 84, 89, 133, 147, 409, 416, 426, 896, and 904), and Bryson is editor of *Virginia Law Books: Essays and Bibliographies* (no. 924), an encyclopedia of Virginia legal literature.

from outside the U.S.[36] With its strong roots in Spanish and French law, Louisiana is the leading example of overlap between the study of American legal literature and that of legal systems outside of the Anglo-American tradition. The living legacy of Spanish and Mexican law in the American Southwest is another example. In addition, as law developed into a learned profession in the U.S., its practitioners turned to Roman law and the legal literatures of France and Germany for inspiration and solutions to new problems. Some 33 studies of these intersections with foreign legal systems are indexed with the heading "American law – Foreign influences." What has been lacking is comparable inquiry into the influence of Anglo-American law books in other legal cultures, with the exception of Blackstone's *Commentaries*.[37]

This brings us to histories of legal literatures from outside of the Anglo-American common law world. The index reveals a substantial body of English-language scholarship on the transnational legal literatures of Western Europe (Roman law, canon law, and their offspring the European *ius commune*). The majority of it is concerned with the development of legal literature in the Middle Ages, especially the *Corpus Juris Civilis* in Roman law and the *Decretum* of Gratian in canon law, as evidenced by the entries for "Roman law – Corpus Juris Civilis" and "Gratian (active 12th century)." There are some thorough overviews of medieval European legal literature.[38]

---

[36] Supporting the work of these historians are ten studies of private libraries of Louisiana lawyers (nos. 208, 246, 349, 350, 351, 434, 442, 509, 515, and 712).

[37] See Horst Dippel, "Blackstone in Germany" (no. 275), and John Emerson, "Did Blackstone Get the Gallic Shrug?" (no. 309).

[38] See Timothy G. Kearley, "A Survey of Medieval European Law and Legal Literature" (no. 520); Harry Dondorp & Eltjo J. H. Schrage, "The Sources of Medieval Learned Law" (no. 286); J. A. Clarence Smith, *Medieval Law Teachers and Writers: Civilian and Canonist* (no. 183); and Tammo Wallinga, "The Common History of European Legal Scholarship" (no. 934). For Roman law specifically, see the two dated but still useful surveys by Stephen L. Sass (nos. 806-807), and Kate Wallach's concise summary in *Bibliographical History of Louisiana Civil Law Sources* (no. 931). All of these cite essential foreign-language works.

24

Unfortunately there is nothing comparable for the early modern period.[39]

International law also figures prominently, dominated by works on Hugo Grotius, considered by many to be the father of modern international law. A series of bibliographic surveys by Peter Macalister-Smith and Joachim Schwietzke (nos. 577-581) supply useful outlines of the literature up through the 19th century.

Among the legal literatures of the nations of Western Europe, Spain's has received the most attention in English-language scholarship. This is not surprising, given the legacy of Spanish law in Louisiana and the American Southwest and its continued relevance in issues such as water rights, mineral rights, and land titles. [40] Recently, the dissemination of law books in Spain's colonial empire has been at the center of a research program on the history of the law book spearheaded by the Max Planck Institute for Legal History and Legal Theory.[41]

French and Dutch law make respectable showings in the checklist,[42] although we have located only a single stand-

---

[39] Good starting points are Douglas J. Osler, "A Survey of the Roman-Dutch Law" (no. 694), Osler's introduction in volume 1 of *Jurisprudence of the Baroque* (no. 695), and the review of *Jurisprudence of the Baroque* by Alain A. Wijffels (no. 962).

[40] See especially Peter L. Reich, "Siete Partidas in My Saddlebags: The Transmission of Hispanic Law from Antebellum Louisiana to Texas and California" (no. 772). John Thomas Vance's *The Background of Hispanic-American Law: Legal Sources and Juridical Literature of Spain* (no. 922) provides a detailed historical survey of Spanish legal literature. The section on "Bibliographical Sources" ranges far beyond Spanish sources, becoming in effect an essay on bibliographic sources of European law from the early modern period onward. For a compact treatment of Spanish legal literature, see Kate Wallach's *Bibliographical History of Louisiana Civil Law Sources* (no. 931).

[41] See nos. 59, 109, 110, 245, 303, 465, 779, and 805.

[42] For an overview of French legal literature, see Wallach (no. 931), as well as Jean Caswell and Ivan Sipkov, *The Coutumes of France in the Library of Congress* (no. 172). For Dutch law, see Osler's essay on Roman-Dutch law (no. 694).

alone historical study in English of the *Code Civil*, one of the most influential works in all of world legal history.[43] English-language studies of German and Italian legal literatures are very slim. Germany and Italy produced enormous bodies of influential legal literature. Cities like Venice, Milan, Frankfurt, and Leipzig were important centers of legal publishing throughout the Renaissance and early modern periods. The lack of English-language guides to these literatures – their authors, their concerns, their development – puts researchers and librarians without the requisite language skills at a disadvantage.

Beyond Western Europe, the situation is even more dire, and the need just as critical. Particularly challenging are the legal literatures rendered in non-roman scripts. For the legal systems in the vast regions of the world outside of Western Europe and North America, the only available guide to their literatures is the indispensable *Library of Congress Law Library: An Illustrated Guide* (no. 554), the only single-volume guide to the world's legal literatures.[44] Its scope is limited only by the breadth of the library's enormous holdings. If you seek general guides to the legal literatures of Africa, East Asia, South Asia, Eastern Europe, Scandinavia, or Russia, of indigenous peoples, of Islamic or Jewish law, it remains to date the only book to turn to.

However, even *Library of Congress Law Library: An Illustrated Guide* has gaps. It has nothing on Latin American legal literature. Our index points to 24 items that address Latin American law, but almost all of them are concerned with colonial Latin America and the literature's connections with U.S. law.[45] And what of the legal literature of the Ottoman

[43] Alain A. Wijffels, "Tampering with the Code Civil 1804-2004," (no. 958).

[44] Its chapters on common law systems, Western Europe, Roman law, canon law, and international law are also excellent.

[45] We should again note that the guides to legal literatures of Latin American nations published by the Law Library of Congress between 1917 and 1976, while designed as research guides rather than historical studies, nevertheless contain substantial historical data. There are guides for Mexico, major Caribbean

Empire, which dominated southeastern Europe and the Middle East for centuries? All these gaps (and they aren't the only ones) represent opportunities for making substantial contributions for Anglophone readers and researchers, especially those pursuing interests in the legacy of colonialism, globalization, and the dissemination of legal knowledge.

Legal genres

Thanks to the fundamental importance of precedent in the common law, case reporting has been by far the most studied genre of law books in English-language scholarship. The vast majority of the 135 works cited under "Case reports" in the index deal with English case reports (66) and American ones (55). A welcome few address the case reporting literature of continental Europe (nos. 21, 22, 176, 277, 399, 474, 866, and 964). Much of the best writing on English and European case reports can be found in three volumes of collected works: *Authorities in Early Modern Law Courts* (2021), *Case Law in the Making: The Techniques and Methods of Judicial Records and Law Reports* (1997), and *Law Reporting in Britain* (1995).[46] For American case reports, the most useful summaries of the pre-electronic era are those by Joseph L. Gerken (no. 366, chapter 2), Erwin C. Surrency (no. 886) and Thomas J. Young, Jr. (no. 994); for the transformation of case reporting from print to digital, see the articles by Robert C. Berring (nos. 74-77). No one has yet attempted a comprehensive, in-depth history of American law reporting.

Treatises have received a large share of attention from historians of legal literature in the last century. One of the entries, A. W. B. Simpson's "The Rise and Fall of the Legal Treatise: Legal Principles and the Forms of Legal Literature"

---

nations (Cuba, the Dominican Republic, and Haiti), and most South American nations, but none for Central America. Searching the Library of Congress online catalog for "Guide to the law and legal literature of" will bring up the relevant titles, including downloadable digitized copies.

[46] See Appendix 2 for full citations, including item numbers for the individual chapters included in the checklist.

(no. 843), is perhaps the most-cited English-language work on the history of law books. There are a substantial number of works on international law treatises (again, dominated by recent work on Hugo Grotius), and a decent number of works on Roman and canon law treatises. An indispensable reference work for the leading treatises in the Western world is *The Formation and Transmission of Western Legal Culture: 150 Books That Made the Law in the Age of Printing* (no. 347), with contributions from leading legal historians. Works that address the treatise literatures of individual European nations would be welcome additions.

Some readers may be unfamiliar with one genre of legal literature, institutional works, although it includes two of the most famous, influential, and frequently published titles in all of legal literature, the *Institutes* of Justinian[47] and William Blackstone's *Commentaries on the Laws of England*.[48] Institutional works are a hybrid between treatises and textbooks. They can be defined as works that use a simple and reasonably logical structure, adapted from Justinian's *Institutes*, to give a comprehensive but elementary treatment of a whole system of law, aimed at law students and others not necessarily familiar with law.[49] Comparative legal historians have argued strenuously for their consideration as a distinct genre, and for their role in the formation of the modern nation-state. Articles by John W. Cairns (no. 160), Klaus Luig (no. 574), and Alan Watson (no. 940) are essential introductions to the genre. They are among 52 works on the genre cited in the index.

While trial accounts of the 19th century have received considerable attention, aided by some outstanding bibliographies,[50] the genre retains considerable potential for further re-

---

[47] Promulgated by the Roman Emperor Justinian in 533; first printed edition, Mainz: Peter Schoeffer, 1468.

[48] First printed Oxford: Clarendon Press, 1765-1769.

[49] John W. Cairns, "Blackstone, an English Institutist: Legal Literature and the Rise of the Nation State" (no. 160), at 327.

[50] Thomas M. McDade, *The Annals of Murder: A Bibliography of Books and*

search. Up to now there has been very little English-language scholarship on trial accounts outside of the English-speaking world. Trial accounts are particularly valuable for capturing the voices and treatment of traditionally marginalized communities, for measuring the application of economic and social power, and for understanding the general public's views about law and the legal system.

In sheer number of titles, law dissertations and related academic publications (debates, inaugural lectures, eulogies, and more) churned out in the universities of northern Europe in the 17th and 18th centuries represent the largest genre in all of legal literature. The largest collection of them, around 100,000 titles, is at the Max Planck Institute for Legal History and Legal Theory.[51] They include some of the earliest publications by Europe's leading intellectuals, including Gottfried Leibniz and Immanuel Kant, and provide maps of discipleship in the German and Dutch legal academies. Dissertations were a lucrative source of income for printers, and a financial burden for law students.[52] Yet there is precious little to guide English-speaking readers through this morass, aside from the two articles by Luca Scholz (nos. 815-816) and a cataloging guide by Susan Karpuk (no. 516).

Another prominent genre in early modern Europe that has so far been overlooked in English-language scholarship is notary manuals.[53] Notaries constituted a distinct legal

---

Pamphlets on American Murders from Colonial Times to 1900 (no. 610); Paul Finkelman, *Slavery in the Courtroom: An Annotated Bibliography of American Cases* (no. 328).

[51] Luca Scholz, "A Distant Reading of Legal Dissertations from German Universities in the Seventeenth Century" (no. 816), at 302.

[52] See Andrew Pettegree & Arthur der Weduwen, "What Was Published in the Seventeenth-century Dutch Republic?", *Livre - Revue Historique* 2018, http://livre.societebibliographique.fr/2018-01, at 17-19.

[53] For general works on notaries, see Laurie Nussdorfer, *Brokers of Public Trust: Notaries in Early Modern Rome* (Baltimore: Johns Hopkins University Press, 2009), and W. W. Smithers, "History of the French Notarial System," *University of Pennsylvania Law Review* 60, no. 1 (Oct. 1911): 19-38.

profession with roots going back to the late Roman Empire, responsible for drafting legal instruments and a host of other tasks. Notary manuals, amalgams of procedure guide and form book, circulated widely in the Middle Ages and became a staple of early printers. In 16th-century Italy alone, printers published manuals by at least a dozen different authors, all appearing in multiple editions. Notary manuals would seem to offer resources for histories of law practice, documentary evidence, book publishing, recordkeeping practices, and even plagiarism (since authors or their publishers copied freely from others). At the least, a bibliographic guide to early modern notary manuals would be welcome.

Legal topics

In comparison with the other subject heading categories, there are comparatively few works in the checklist that focus on specific fields of law (60, to be exact). The literature of criminal law, both professional and popular, is the subject of twenty entries, in which the work of Thomas M. McDade, the maestro of American murder trials, figures prominently. Maritime law is well served: W. Senior's "Early Writers on Maritime Law" (no. 827) is a century old but has aged well, and Daniel R. Coquillette's *The Civilian Writers of Doctors' Commons* (no. 218) provides a thorough study of English writers on maritime law.

The evolution of U.S. legal research is thoroughly documented in Joseph Gerken's book (no. 366), its historical literature is covered in Steven M. Barkan's review essay (no. 46), and its digital transformation is explored in the influential articles by Robert C. Berring (nos. 74-77) and Richard A. Danner (nos. 240, 242, and 243). Where are the equivalent studies of legal research in the U.K. and elsewhere?

One glaring gap is studies of the literature of law reform. For England, there are two substantial monographs for the early modern period,[54] and in "Aspects of Nineteenth-Century Legal Literature," Jon Davies devotes a few pages to "the literature of disaffection."[55] For the United States, we have found no studies focused on the literature of law reform, with the notable exception of Paul Finkelman's bibliography of slavery trials (no. 328). Since the colonial period, vigorous debates have been carried out in the popular press on topics including bankruptcy, court reform, legal education, and much more. Much of the printed material produced by all sides of the labor movement, the women's movement, the civil rights struggle, the Red Scare, and other crusades have dealt with legal issues. Some of the liveliest debates on U.S. constitutional law have taken place in their pages.

Bibliographic genres

This category references 184 entries on the checklist. Anglo-American law is blessed with superb general bibliographies. These include Adams and Averley for the eighteenth century (no. 2), Adams and Davies for the nineteenth century (no. 3), Joseph H. Beale's *Bibliography of Early English Law Books* (no. 58), and Morris Cohen's monumental *Bibliography of Early American Law* (no. 200). For other jurisdictions, there is expectedly less coverage in English, but the checklist features bibliographies for the legal literature of the European continent, indexed by country name, as well as the areas of Roman law (e.g., nos. 206, 806, and 807), canon law (nos. 520, 558, and 721), and international law (e.g., nos. 220-228, 385, 577-581, 771, and 852), the latter with a notable focus on the bibliography of Hugo Grotius's famous *De jure belli ac pacis*. More bibliographies in English on European, and other, jurisdictions would be desirable. It would also be worthwhile

---

[54] Nancy L. Matthews, *William Sheppard, Cromwell's Law Reformer* (no. 603), and Barbara J. Shapiro, *Law Reform in Early Modern England: Crown, Parliament and the Press* (no. 830).

[55] No. 248, at 31-36.

to have a modern guide to the early scholarly bibliographies of European law.[56]

Much else apart from the bibliography of legal systems and the literature of particular countries fits under this category. Exhibition catalogs are an important bibliographic form that is sometimes overlooked. These often document literature in fine-grained ways, and contextualize and relate their component pieces with a sensitivity that reflects the underlying physical exhibits.[57] Catalogs sometimes represent the most detailed form of bibliography, and some have remained mainstays of bibliographic reference. Catalogs for law book exhibitions are well-represented in the checklist.[58] A corollary to exhibition catalogs, as far as value and, more occasionally, underrepresentation in the genre of bibliography, are auction catalogs.[59] Some auction catalogs are essential for the bibliography of a particular field and law is no exception.[60] Finally, library catalogs are a traditional source of bibliography. Although published prior to our cutoff date, *The Catalogue of the Library of Harvard University Law School*, 2 vols. (1909), is still an important resource. Others are also of a general scope and represent useful reference works.[61] As

[56] Such as Martin Lipen's *Bibliotheca realis juridica* (1678), Burkhard Gotthelf Struve's *Bibliotheca iuris selecta* (1703), or Karl Ferdinand Hommel's *Litteratura iuris* (1761).

[57] For example, Michael Widener and Mark S. Weiner, *Law's Picture Books: The Yale Law Library Collection* (no. 948), is the definitive catalog for illustrated law books.

[58] See, in particular, the printed catalogs of exhibits staged at the Yale Law Library (nos. 15, 599, 748, 945, 978); and exhibits staged at the Boston College Law Library (nos. 62-64, 82, 255-262, 264-265).

[59] For example, auction catalogs from Bonhams (nos. 102-104) and Doyle (nos. 288-289) record troves of legal material, deaccessioned by major law libraries, that are bibliographically significant and seldom seen on the market.

[60] See, in particular, the *Illustrated Catalogue of Acts and Laws of the Colony and State of New York and of the Other Original Colonies and States: Constituting the Collection Made by Hon. Russell Benedict, Justice of the Supreme Court of New York* (no. 5).

[61] See the *Catalog of the Hampton L. Carson Collection Illustrative of the*

importantly, scholars have opened new and deeper fields of research by gathering, for example, the legal literatures of American colonies and territories, genres of legal publishing, and libraries.[62] On the checklist, several other non-legal genres also deserve mention. These include comic books and juvenile literature, which both intersect with the law and have received some attention in scholarly print.[63] Further bibliographical work would facilitate a better understanding of the various roles that the law plays in popular culture.

Bibliographic topics

The history of the law book has flourished in the last few decades. On the checklist, "History of the Book" references 34 entries, of which some notable introductions have been published in the last fifteen years.[64] In a similar way, more focused studies on publishing and bookselling have illuminated new paths for research. For work on England, publications have brought a more nuanced understanding of the development of the common law and the important role

Growth of the Common Law, in the Free Library of Philadelphia (no. 352), and Julius Marke's *Catalogue of the Law Collection at New York University: With Selected Annotations* (no. 594).

[62] Among more specific bibliographies, several excellent works of scholarship have brought a wide variety of material to light: Bryson's *Census of Law Books in Colonial Virginia* (no. 138), Cohen and Hamby O'Connor's work on early Supreme Court reports (no. 199), Eller's *The William Blackstone Collection in the Yale Law Library: A Bibliographical Catalogue* (no. 306), and Laeuchli's *Bibliographical Catalog of William Blackstone* (no. 547), are classics.

[63] See William A. Hilyerd, "Hi Superman, I'm a Lawyer: A Guide to Attorneys (and Other Legal Professionals) Portrayed in American Comic Books: 1910-2007" (no. 425), and Morris L. Cohen, *Juvenile Jurisprudence: Law in Children's Literature* (no. 202).

[64] In particular, see Angela Fernandez, "Legal History as the History of Legal Texts" (no. 322), Antonio Manuel Hespanha, "Form and Content in Early Modern Legal Books: Bridging the Gap Between Material Bibliography and the History of Legal Thought" (no. 419), Michael H. Hoeflich, "Legal History and the History of the Book: Variations on a Theme" (no. 432), and Henrike Manuwald, "Book History" (no. 592), for several thought-provoking introductions.

printing has played in that long-term process.[65] Studies of continental printing and bookselling have resulted in similar work for those traditions, with a focus on printing, though fewer are available in English.[66] Studies of the same for American law are well represented on the checklist, both in broad and narrow scope (e.g., nos. 177, 519, and 560). Studies of law book publishing in the major European publishing centers of Venice, Lyon, Paris, Frankfurt, and Nuremberg would be welcome. Further studies of American legal booksellers and printers, and the circulation of American law books in the trade, would likewise be of value to librarians, students, and researchers.

A series of specific topics in book history, of growing interest and importance to scholars and students of legal history, are also included under this category. Scholarly work on "paratexts" has focused first on glosses and apparatus to medieval law books, typically in their manuscript forms.[67] Gero Dolezalek, in particular, has done extraordinary work in English in this area (see nos. 278, 279, 281, and 284). The entry for paratexts also references work on the prefaces and prologues of law books; these have provided a number of stimulating insights into their function as an integral part of legal texts, as reflections of their authors' methodology

[65]   See Tariq Baloch, "Law Booksellers and Printers as Agents of Unchange" (no. 45), Richard J. Ross, "The Commoning of the Common Law: The Renaissance Debate over Printing English Law, 1520-1640" (no. 797), and Ian Williams, "'He Creditted More the Printed Booke': Common Lawyers' Receptivity to Print, c. 1550-1640" (no. 967).

[66]   See Laura Beck Varela, "The Diffusion of Law Books in Early Modern Europe: A Methodological Approach" (no. 59), William Kemp, "Where and How to Print the Florentine Pandects: Paris, Basle, Lyons, Venice or Florence?" (no. 526), Maria Alessandra Panzanelli Fratoni, "Printing the Law in the 15th Century with a Focus on *Corpus iuris civilis* and the Works of Bartolus de Saxoferrato" (no. 706), and Steven W. Rowan, "Jurists and the Printing Press in Germany: The First Century" (no. 801).

[67]   For interesting and important comments, see Mario Ascheri and Paola Maffei, "Juridical Late Medieval Paratexts and the Growth of European Jurisprudence" (no. 12), and Emanuele Conte, "The Centre and the Margins of the Jungle of Glossed Manuscripts" (no. 211).

and intentions, and into their relationship to the doctrinal content of books.[68] An exhibition catalog by Laurel Davis and Melissa Grasso (no. 265) considers epigraphs in law books, a field of inquiry that, like prefaces and prologues, deserves more study. Among bibliographic topics are also studies on typography and design, another fascinating though still relatively understudied area in legal history.[69]

A bibliographic topic that has received somewhat more study, at least for U.S. legal literature, is the organization of legal information. Joseph Gerken's *The Invention of Legal Research* (no. 366) is an indispensable historical overview. Citators have been thoroughly studied by Patti Ogden (no. 672) and others. Fred Shapiro has situated citation indexes within the broader history of bibliometrics (no. 831). The influential series of articles by Robert C. Berring (nos. 74-77) explore the ways in which the vast indexes created by West Publishing and others profoundly shape the "thinkable thoughts" about the law. One wishes for comparable English-language studies on the organization of legal information outside of the Anglo-American world.

Finally, illustrations are an important and appealing phenomenon in historical law books. These images, more common than might be imagined and serving a wide range of purposes, interact with legal texts and doctrinal teachings in complex ways; and have started to receive their due in recent years. On the checklist, see the comprehensive exhibition catalog by Michael Widener and Mark Weiner, *Law's Picture Books: The Yale Law Library Collection* (no. 948), Widener, "From Law Book to Legal Book: The Origin of a Species"

---

[68] Gisela Drossbach, "Prefaces in Canon Law Books" (no. 294), George Garnett, "'The Ould Fields': Law and History in the Prefaces to Sir Edward Coke's *Reports*" (no. 365), Huw Pryce, "The Prologues to the Welsh Lawbooks" (no. 752), Wouter Werner, "Prefaces and Authorship in International Law: The Example of Vitoria's *De Indis*" (no. 942).

[69] For example, Luciana Devoti, "A Medieval Puzzle: The 'Architecture' of the Page in Manuscripts and Incunabula of the Codex Justinianus" (no. 269), and Kasia Solon Cristobal, "From Law in Blackletter to Blackletter Law" (no. 856).

(no. 950), Peter Goodrich, *Legal Emblems and the Art of Law: Obiter Depicta as the Vision of Governance* (no. 377), and Goodrich, "The Emblem Book and Common Law" (no. 378). Other studies of law book illustrations have traditionally focused on manuscript images, including several good recent contributions by Anthony Musson (nos. 656-659).

Libraries – private, professional and academic – is another area in this category for which there is a rich body of scholarly work. Notably, more scholarship has been produced on private legal libraries in America (e.g., nos. 442, 452, 453, 515, 633) than in England and Great Britain (e.g. nos. 814, 858, 868). This is perhaps in part because of the relative importance of private libraries in this country over a long period, and their status as a good, sometimes surprising, index of the diffusion of the common law and continental legal traditions in America. The checklist features somewhat fewer studies of academic and professional libraries, but here, too, can be found important works that highlight well- and lesser-known histories and collections, many of which deserve further attention.[70] For England, Alain Wijffels has produced several useful pieces (nos. 952-954, 957). Studies of libraries in Europe and Latin America are abundant in their native languages, but there are few in English, as the index demonstrates.

Names

William Blackstone is, unsurprisingly, the most thoroughly studied legal author in the checklist, followed closely by Hugo Grotius. John Selden and Sir Edward Coke have also been given well deserved attention.

Three bio-bibliographical works are worth mentioning once again. *The Formation and Transmission of Western Legal Culture: 150 Books That Made the Law in the Age of*

---

[70] For example, *Catalog of the Roman Law Collection of the Columbia Law School Library* (no. 206), Joseph A. Custer, "Case Western University Law School Library: 125 Years" (no. 236), and Scott Hamilton Dewey, "Growing Pains: The History of the UCLA Law Library, 1949-2000." (no. 270).

Printing (no. 347), previously mentioned, is described by one reviewer as "A monumental collective undertaking … partly an exercise in disciplinary history and partly in book history."[71] J. A. Clarence Smith's *Medieval Law Teachers and Writers, Civilian and Canonist* (no. 183) remains useful after a half-century, although the Anglicized names are awkward. Frederick C. Hicks's classic *Men and Books Famous in the Law* (no. 422) gives us lively portraits of seven leading English and American legal writers: John Cowell, Edward Coke, Thomas Littleton, William Blackstone, James Kent, Edward Livingston, and Henry Wheaton.

In the index readers will find 149 headings for individual authors, publishers, and booksellers, from the famous to the obscure. What follows is a wish list, suggestions for future research.

For the second half of the 16th century, one man, Richard Tottel (died 1594), dominated common law printing in England. Yet to date the only study devoted to Tottel is a 1932 article by H. J. Byrom (no. 157). While Byrom's article is based on thorough research and remains quite useful, many of the bibliographic details are now outdated, and much of Tottel's law publishing is passed over. Until the advent of West Publishing in the late 19th century, no other publisher had a greater impact on the literature of the common law. Hasn't the time come for a full-dress study of Tottel?

A number of English authors have yet to receive any substantial attention: Edmund Saunders (died 1683), the colorful rags-to-riches barrister whose case reports served as a textbook for pleading for two centuries; Ferdinando Pulton (1536-1618), whose Catholic religion forced him into a career as a compiler of statutes; and John Brydall (born 1635), vocal defender of the royal prerogative. In two recent posts on *In Custodia Legis*, the blog of the Law Library of Congress, Nathan Dorn describes two American authors deserving study: Simon Greenleaf (1783-1853), reporter of Maine decisions,

---

[71] "From the Literature," *Jus Gentium* 3, no. 1 (Jan. 2018), at 376.

Dane Professor at Harvard Law School, and author of the first American citation index;[72] and Francis Hilliard (1806-1878), "a little-known 19th century author, who made great strides toward creating a library of American law."[73] There are certainly others.

In medieval canon law, Giovanni d'Andrea (1270?-1348) was the most respected and prolific author of his time, and unusual for a canon lawyer, a layman, whose career was cut short by the Black Death. In Germany, worthy candidates include Benedikt Carpzov (1595-1666), considered the founder of German legal science, or Karl Ferdinand Hommel (1722-1781), law professor, bibliographer, and one of those rare legal authors with a sense of humor. For France, one would like to know more about Jean Chappuis (active ca. 1500), who would embed his name in acrostics in the Roman and canon law texts he edited, or Robert-Joseph Pothier (1699-1772), the authority on commercial law who was widely read in early America. For Italy, there is not yet an English-language study of Prospero Farinacci (1554-1618), the colorful author of the most influential criminal law treatise of the Renaissance. These are only a few of the many legal authors awaiting study.

As regards American legal publishing, West Publishing has received the lion's share of scholarly attention, and deservedly so, but a number of major 19th-century legal publishers await study, such as Little Brown of Boston, T. & J. W. Johnson of Philadelphia, the Gilbert Book Company of St. Louis, or Callaghan & Company of Chicago.

[72]   https://blogs.loc.gov/law/2022/09/collection-highlights-simon-greenleaf-and-the-first-american-legal-citation-index/

[73]   https://blogs.loc.gov/law/2023/11/collection-highlights-the-many-lawbooks-of-francis-hilliard/

Histories of Legal Literature, 1921-2022: A Few of Our Favorite Things

As the checklist grew to 998 entries, it became clear that it would be impossible to annotate each entry in a reasonable amount of time. Instead of annotated entries, we opted for a detailed subject index. In addition, we endeavored to mention significant works in the preceding text and footnotes.

In the same spirit, we offer three "top ten" annotated lists of our favorite titles from the checklist. The first, "Top Ten Reference Works," is our consensus on ten essential reference works. Our criteria include reputation, usefulness, and a balance of coverage. The other two are our individual favorites; the criteria are entirely subjective and personal. The lists are arranged by checklist item number.

Top Ten Reference Works

58. Beale, Joseph H. *Bibliography of Early English Law Books*. Cambridge, MA: Harvard University Press, 1926. [With] Anderson, Robert B. *A Supplement to Beale's Bibliography of Early English Law Books*. Cambridge, MA: Harvard University Press, 1943.

> The benchmark work for identifying English legal works published from the beginning of printing in England to 1600. "No better tribute to the memory of James Barr Ames could be made than a scholarly and carefully compiled volume of the early printed books on that early law of England... This book will be of use to all students of the law."[74]

---

[74] Margaret C. Klinglesmith, Review of *A Bibliography of Early English Law Books* by Joseph Henry Beale, *University of Pennsylvania Law Review and*

200. Cohen, Morris L. *Bibliography of Early American Law.* 6 vols., and 2003 supplement. Buffalo, NY: William S. Hein & Co., 1998.

"As an enormous, comprehensive, systematically organized, and easily accessible grid of a vast number of primary sources in the field of American legal history, Morris L. Cohen's *Bibliography of Early American Law* not only is a scholarly classic in its own right, but also lays out the evidentiary base ... for dozens of other classic scholarly essays, articles, dissertations, and monographs yet to be written."[75]

347. *The Formation and Transmission of Western Legal Culture: 150 Books That Made the Law in the Age of Printing* (Serge Dauchy et al., eds.; Cham, Switzerland: Springer, 2016).

"A monumental collective undertaking with nearly as many contributors as books chosen for inclusion, each working to a standard outline and within a strict word limit ... This is partly an exercise in disciplinary history and partly in book history ... A veritable encyclopedia of western legal history."[76]

395. Grossman, George S. *Legal Research: Historical Foundations of the Electronic Age.* New York: Oxford University Press, 1994.

"George Grossman ... has written a readable book with an intriguing hypothesis. He proposes that the best preparation for doing legal research in today's hightech computer environment is to return to historical

---

American Law Register 75, no. 5 (Mar., 1927): 482-83.

[75] Daniel A. Cohen, "In Praise of Praise of Morris L. Cohen's *Bibliography of Early American Law*" (no. 191), at 28.

[76] *Jus Gentium* 3, no. 1 (Jan. 2018), at 376.

sources in order to appreciate the very nature of legal information."[77]

547. Laeuchli, Ann Jordan. *A Bibliographical Catalog of William Blackstone*. Buffalo, N.Y.: Published for Yale Law Library by William S. Hein & Co., 2015.

William Blackstone, whose *Commentaries* remain the single most important work in the history of Anglo-American law, earned a bibliography as exhaustive as that produced by Laeuchli, which extended the earlier bibliography of Catherine Spicer Eller (no. 306). "The 266 entries in Eller included only the Blackstone collection at Yale, while Laeuchli's 672 entries cover all editions of Blackstone's works published in the Roman alphabet, plus biographies, criticisms, catalogs, prospectuses, exhibitions, microtexts, and electronic resources."[78]

554. Law Library of Congress. *Library of Congress Law Library: An Illustrated Guide*. Washington, D.C.: Library of Congress, 2005.

The only single-volume history of the world's legal literature, authoritative, clearly written, and lavishly illustrated. For many of the world's legal literatures, it remains the only English-language guide; Latin American legal literature is the only notable gap.

610. McDade, Thomas M. *The Annals of Murder: A Bibliography of Books and Pamphlets on American Murders from Colonial Times to 1900*. Norman, OK: University of Oklahoma Press, 1961.

[77] *American Journal of Legal History* 39, no. 3 (July 1995), at 389.

[78] Michael Widener, "Ann Laeuchli's Bibliographical Catalog of William Blackstone," Lillian Goldman Law Library announcement, October 21, 2014. Accessed January 24, 2024: https://library.law.yale.edu/news/ann-laeuchlis-bibliographical-catalog-william-blackstone.

42

> "To book people dealing with the literature of American crime, one reference work is of towering importance: Thomas McDade's bibliography, *The Annals of Murder*. ... Indeed, it is so well conceived and executed, and so engaging in its own right, that it might fairly be said to be one of the finest genre bibliographies in American book collecting."[79]

843. Simpson, A. W. B. "The Rise and Fall of the Legal Treatise: Legal Principles and the Forms of Legal Literature." *University of Chicago Law Review* 48, no. 3 (Summer 1981): 632-679.

> In outlining the development of the Anglo-American legal treatise, Simpson aims to establish "the close relation between the forms of legal literature and lawyers' ideas of what they are doing, and of the appropriate way for jurists to behave" (p. 633). One of the most-cited works in English on the history of legal literature.

892. Sweet & Maxwell. *A Legal Bibliography of the British Commonwealth of Nations*. 8 vols. London: Sweet & Maxwell, 1955-1964.

> A work noted for its scope and usefulness. Two volumes cover historical English law up through the mid-twentieth century, and the additional volumes cover the common law as applied across other Commonwealth jurisdictions.

934. Wallinga, Tammo. "The Common History of European Legal Scholarship." *Erasmus Law Review* 4, no. 1 (2011): 3-20. https://doi.org/10.5553/ELR221026712011004001002

> The most comprehensive yet concise summary of the legal literature of Western Europe.

---

[79] Patterson Smith, "Thomas McDade and the *Annals of Murder*" (no. 851), at 1613.

Widener's Top Ten

29. Baker, John H. *Monuments of Endlesse Labours: English Canonists and Their Work, 1300-1900.* London: Hambledon Press, 1998.

> These bio-bibliographical essays are lively and sympathetic portraits of English canonists, "an attempt to set them, in a non-technical way, in some kind of context" (p. ix). The writing is Baker at his best.

45. Baloch, Tariq. "Law Booksellers and Printers as Agents of Unchange." *Cambridge Law Journal* 66 (2007): 385-421.

> Baloch demonstrates how publishers shaped the common law, much to the law's detriment: "the monopolistic business practices employed and enjoyed especially by the law book trade ... created a market in which it was difficult to publish new works" (p. 421), the prime example being Blackstone's *Commentaries*.

56. Baum, Marsha L., and Christian G. Fritz. "American Constitution-Making: The Neglected State Constitutional Sources." *Hastings Constitutional Law Quarterly* 27, no. 2 (Winter 2000): 199-242.

> By marshalling an impressive array of data including publishing history, evidence of ownership, and physical size, the authors show how a seemingly mundane and *textually* insignificant genre (antebellum compilations of U.S. state constitutions) influenced the writers of early state constitutions and the general public. It is an excellent example of the relevance of book history to substantive issues in legal history.

202. Cohen, Morris L. *Juvenile Jurisprudence: Law in Children's Literature: An Exhibition Drawing in Part on the Betsy Beinecke Shirley Collection of American Children's Literature, January 30 through April 11, 2003.* New Haven, CT: Beinecke Rare Book and Manuscript Library, Yale University, 2003.

44

> Early in my career I considered and then rejected the
> idea that children's books could have much relevance
> to the history of legal literature. Morris Cohen proves
> how wrong I was.[80]

688. Osler, Douglas J. "Text and Technology." *Rechtshistorisches Journal* 14 (1995): 309-331.

> This is one of a group of articles[81] in which Osler
> addresses "the Great Myth of Print ... that whereas all
> manuscripts are different, all editions are the same ...
> and since all editions are the same, any old edition will
> do" (p. 322-323). This myth, he argues, has infected
> the practices of both legal history and the bibliography
> of early printed legal texts, with dire consequences for
> both, and offers his remedies. Osler's terse summary of
> the economics of early printing is memorable: "paper
> was very expensive, and labor was very cheap" (p.
> 318).

834. Shapiro, Fred R., & Julie Graves Krishnaswami. "The
Secret History of the Bluebook." *Minnesota Law Review* 100,
no. 4 (Apr. 2016): 1563-1598.

> First, full disclosure: Shapiro and Graves Krishnaswami
> are friends and former colleagues, and I am named in
> the acknowledgments. That being said, I like a good
> detective story, and this article is an excellent piece of
> bibliographic detective work on the origins of one of
> the most famous (or infamous) legal reference books of
> modern times.

856. Solon Cristobal, Kasia. "From Law in Blackletter to
Blackletter Law." *Law Library Journal* 108, no. 2 (2016):
181-216.

---

[80] See Michael Widener, 'Morris Cohen and the Art of Book Collecting" (no. 947).

[81] See also nos. 681-683.

Taking a deep dive into "how the law looks matters, aside from what it says" (p. 215), the author argues that "letter shapes in legal texts have played an outsized role in the history of the law that merits separate consideration" (p. 185), in another outstanding application of book history to legal history.

882. Stotter, Lawrence H. *To Put Asunder: The Laws of Matrimonial Strife; An Introduction to the Seminal Anglo-American Literature and Laws of Domestic Relations Up to the Year 1900, with Supporting Bibliography and Comments.* Berkeley: Regent Press, 2011.

This beautifully designed volume is both a history of family law and a catalog of the field's historical literature by one of its leading practitioners. It is an example of the contributions that a knowledgeable and dedicated collector can make to scholarship.

940. Watson, Alan. "The Importance of 'Nutshells'." *American Journal of Comparative Law* 42, no. 1 (Winter 1994): 1-23.

This article reshaped my understanding of legal literature. Watson defines nutshells as "books written as teaching manuals ... for beginning law students or to instruct non-lawyers in the elements of the law" (p.1), such as Justinian's *Institutes* or Blackstone's *Commentaries*. "As a result they determine forever the pattern and parameters of lawyers' thought" (p. 18). In other words, if you want to understand how lawyers thought, don't look at sophisticated treatises; look at the nutshells.

979. Winroth, Anders. "Gratian and His Book: How a Medieval Teacher Changed European Law and Religion." *Oxford Journal of Law and Religion* 10, no. 1 (2021): 1-15.

In an eloquent and affectionate essay, Winroth explains how Gratian's *Decretum*, as originally conceived, was not a compilation of canon law but rather an innovative textbook, designed to teach Gratian's students to think

46

like lawyers (much like modern casebooks). Gratian also set out many of the foundational principles of modern due process.

Greenwood's Top Ten

19. Baker, John H. "Coke's Note-Books and the Sources of his Reports." *Cambridge Law Journal* 30, no. 1 (Apr. 1972): 59-86.

Baker offers a deeper understanding of the making of law reports, here in an early study of Edward Coke, perhaps England's greatest jurist and most influential reporter. Early modern case reports drew from oral tradition, manuscript and print, and all relied on personal industry, interests, and chance. The article gives good insight into Coke's own practices in the midst of his busy career.

439. Hoeflich, Michael H. "Auctions and the Distribution of Law Books in Antebellum America." *Proceedings of the American Antiquarian Society* 113, no. 1 (Apr. 2003): 135-161.

One of Michael Hoeflich's less-cited pieces, this is full of his usual acumen and touches familiar, important themes: how law books have circulated and how legal knowledge was acquired in early America. As a work on the history of the law book trade, via auctions, it is all the more useful because "few business records of antebellum law booksellers and publishers survive" (p. 140).

513. Kantorowicz, Hermann. *Studies in the Glossators of the Roman Law: Newly Discovered Writings of the Twelfth Century.* Cambridge, UK: Cambridge University Press, 1938.

Kantorowicz, a refugee from Nazi Germany to the United States and England, was a towering scholar of medieval and modern law. His contributions to criminal law, jurisprudence and legal history are still influential. His preeminent English-language study of medieval Roman law teachers and their writings has a wealth of information on the origins of later European legal thought.

532. Keynes, Simon. "The Engraved Facsimile by John Pine (1733) of the 'Canterbury' Magna Carta (1215)." In *English Legal History and Its Sources: Essays in Honour of Sir John Baker* (David Ibbetson et al.; eds.; Cambridge, UK: Cambridge University Press, 2019), 223-244.

Keynes's piece, detailing a famed facsimile reproduction of a damaged copy of *Magna Carta*, is a microhistory on how legal texts can be artfully and expensively commemorated. Surrounded by myth, *Magna Carta* and similar texts have been woven into the fabric of national cultures.

535. Kisch, Guido. "Juridicial Lexicography and the Reception of Roman Law." *Seminar* (Jurist) 2 (1944): 51-81.

Roman law exerted enormous influence on the European continent, where it had to be rendered into the terms of indigenous regional laws. Dictionaries with parallel definitions ensured that this would be possible. Kisch's study is an excellent look at how legal concepts have been translated across space and time.

646. Monballyu, Jos. "Joos de Damhouder, an Internationally Influential Jurist from Bruges." In *The Art of Law: Three Centuries of Justice Depicted* (Stefan Huygebaert *et al.*, eds.; Tielt: Lannoo, 2018), 106-119.

Illustrated law books were overlooked until relatively recently, when more attention has been paid to the didactic and symbolic importance of images in law books. This interesting English-language study by Monballyu sheds light on the career of a renowned jurist whose magnum opus relied on lavish images to convey the didactic and moral dimensions of his criminal law handbook – and to sell copies.

672. Ogden, Patti J. "'Mastering the Lawless Science of Our Law': A Story of Legal Citation Indexes." *Law Library Journal* 85, no. 1 (1993): 1-48.

Ogden's study is the best introduction to the history of legal citators in America. The history is important and interesting: another case in which new forms of books and information have guided the law itself, in this instance the modern development and dimensions of legal precedent.

797. Ross, Richard J. "The Commoning of the Common Law: The Renaissance Debate over Printing English Law, 1520-1640." *University of Pennsylvania Law Review* 146, no. 2 (1998): 323-461.

Ross's work (along with that of others) heralded the turn toward book history in legal history. His classic article investigates why printing law was advocated and opposed in England, against contested social and political backgrounds. It shows how disruptive and creative the advent of print was for the law.

861. Stauffer, Jill. "'You people talk from paper': Indigenous Law, Western Legalism, and the Cultural Variability of Law's Materials." *Law Text Culture* 23 (2019), 40-57. https://ro.uow.edu.au/ltc/vol23/iss1/4

Taking a different perspective on legal texts, Stauffer examines how for indigenous Americans law may be read and inscribed in forms of storytelling, songs and symbolic cultural artifacts, which European-based systems need to recognize and take into account, particularly in court.

948. Widener, Michael, & Mark S. Weiner. *Law's Picture Books: The Yale Law Library Collection*. Clark, NJ: Talbot Publishing, 2017.

Widener and Weiner's catalog, a companion to their exhibition at the Grolier Club, is the best collection of illustrated law books available. Included among the sumptuous entries is an extraordinary variety of images: from symbols of the law's majesty, to diagrams used to teach and explain, to social and legal advocacy conveyed through cartoons. It is a compendium for students and researchers and a feast for the eyes.

Postscript: Late arrivals

Although we have made no concerted effort to compile additions to the field after our cutoff date of 2022, we wish to mention a few notable publications that have appeared since then.

Two of these are in a field that is a personal favorite of ours, legal iconography. In *The Tree of Legal Knowledge: Imagining Blackstone's Commentaries*,[82] John V. Orth has produced one of the very few works on American legal illustrations,[83] as well as an extremely impressive example of bibliographic detective work. Héléna D. M. Lagréou's "Hung up on Judas: A Case Study on the Pragmatic Usage of Religious Iconography in Legal Manuscripts of the Institutiones"[84] is the latest addition to a large body of work on the illustrations in medieval law manuscripts, produced by authors such as Robert Gibbs, Susan L'Engle, and Anthony Musson.

American legal bibliography is nurtured by yet another contribution from Joel Fishman, *Bibliography of Pennsylvania Legal Treatises*.[85]

Other works continue to expand the history of legal literature beyond the confines of Western Europe and North America. For Russia, we have William E. Butler and V. S. Ivanenko's *The Saint Petersburg School of International Law A Bio-Bibliographical Study (Petrine Russia to the 1920s)*,[86]

---

[82] Singapore: Springer, 2023. The book concludes the work that Orth began in no. 676.

[83] See also nos. 251 and 438.

[84] *Eikón Imago* 12 (2023): 29-43; available online at https://doi.org/10.5209/eiko.83411.

[85] Getzville, N.Y.: William S. Hein & Co., 2023.

[86] Clark, NJ: Talbot Publishing, 2023.

and, for China, Taisu Zhang's "The Private Law Influence of the Great Qing Code."[87] Arthur Barrêtto de Almeida Costa's "Citation Networks in Administrative Law Books from the Civil Law World (Nineteenth Century)"[88] is worth mentioning as one of the few applications of bibliometrics to the history of legal literature,[89] and also as a critique of Eurocentric history. The latest volume from the Max Planck Institute for Legal History and Legal Theory focuses on one of the most frequently published books in all of legal literature, Martín de Azpilcueta's *Manual de Confessores*, and its dissemination throughout the Americas and Asia in the early modern period.[90]

---

[87] In *The Making of the Chinese Civil Code* (Hao Jiang & Pietro Sirena, eds.; Cambridge University Press, 2023), 249-268.

[88] *Comparative Legal History* (2023), https://doi.org/10.1080/204967 7X.2023.2270388.

[89] For other examples of bibliometrics applied to the history of legal literature, see nos. 50 (also by Barrêtto de Almeida Costa), 706, and 831.

[90] *The Production of Knowledge of Normativity in the Age of the Printing Press: Martín de Azpilcueta's Manual de Confessores from a Global Perspective* (Manuela Bragagnolo, ed.; Leiden: Brill, 2024). The Max Planck Institute deserves our applause and praise for making the entire volume accessible open-access, at https://brill.com/display/title/69299.

Notes to the Index

The index of 392 subject headings and 149 name headings provides access to the 998 numbered entries in the checklist that follows. The headings are designed to promote and facilitate comparative studies across jurisdictional boundaries. In addition, the index serves as a bibliometric, describing the contours of the existing English-language scholarship on the history of legal literature, highlighting both strengths and gaps, and hopefully inspiring researchers to fill some of those gaps.

The index headings fall into seven categories:

1. *Bodies of law*: 179 headings that point to histories of the legal literature of individual nations (American law, Dutch law, etc.) or entire regions (Asian law, Scandinavian law, etc.), as well as the literature of transnational legal systems (British Commonwealth law, canon law, international law, Islamic law, Roman law).

2. *Legal literature genres*: 79 headings for studies of traditional genres in the field of law: abridgments and digests, bibliographies, case reports, citators, constitutions, dictionaries, handbooks and manuals, institutional works, periodicals, statutes, textbooks, treatises, and trials; as well as the modern format of digital media.

3. *Legal topics*: 16 headings for works dealing with the literature of specific fields of law: civil rights, commercial law, contracts, copyright, criminal law, domestic relations, law reform, legal research, libel, maritime law, medical jurisprudence, slavery, women.

4. *Bibliographic genres*: 43 headings for bibliographic tools dedicated to legal literature (historical bibliographies, auction catalogs, exhibition catalogs, library catalogs), and studies of genres that are not exclusive to law

54

(comics, commonplace books, juvenile works, oral texts, translations).

5. *Bibliographic topics*: 58 headings for works on the field of legal bibliography (its methodology and practice), book and manuscript collectors, censorship, history of the book, illustration, indexing, interleaving, libraries (academic, private, professional, public), manuscript studies, paratexts, publishing and bookselling, typography and design.

6. *Names*: 149 name headings, derived from Library of Congress name authorities, applied to works on specific authors, publishers, and booksellers.

7. *Chronological periods*: 17 headings for "Ancient law" and "Medieval law" (see the definitions below).

Each entry in the checklist has been indexed with as many headings from as many categories as the item warrants, typically between two and eight. Some have only one heading, particularly the studies of individual libraries. A select few, thanks to their wide scope and substantial coverage on a variety of topics, are indexed under ten or more headings (nos. 217, 248, 274, 347, 366, 422, 554, 804, 893, and 924). Appendix 4 gives statistics for the subject headings.

Subheadings have been added to a majority of the main headings. The headings for legal genres also serve as subheadings for bodies of law, and vice versa. For example, no. 1 in the checklist, L. W. Abbott's *Law Reporting in England 1485-1585*, is indexed under both "English law – case reports" and "Case reports – English law," thus facilitating comparative research across genres and bodies of law.

For American law, subheadings for individual states provide access to works on their legal literatures, most prominently those of California, Kentucky, Louisiana, Pennsylvania, Texas, and Virginia.

There are subheadings for three individual works that have played an outsized role in English-language histories of legal literature: *Magna Carta* and Blackstone's *Commentaries* in English law, and the *Corpus Juris Civilis* in Roman law. For studies of another landmark work, the medieval English treatise commonly known as *Bracton*, see the heading for its purported author, "Bracton, Henry de (died 1268)."

The index uses three chronological subheadings. "American law – Pre-Independence" is for works that focus on legal literature in the thirteen North American colonies before they declared independence from England in 1776 and became the United States of America. "Roman law – Ancient" is for works on the literature of Roman law up through the compilation and promulgation of the *Corpus Juris Civilis* by the Roman emperor Justinian in the sixth century. The subheading "medieval" is for works on legal literature from the seventh century up to the advent of printing in 1455. "Medieval law" is also a main topic heading, as a nod to the busy field of medieval studies and as a stimulus for comparative studies. Time constraints and the vigorous debates over historical periodization discouraged us from supplying further chronological subheadings.

Following the checklist itself, which is arranged alphabetically by primary author, is an index of co-authors.

While most of the subject terms are self-explanatory, the following terms deserve clarification.

- *African law*: does not include South African law, which is indexed separately.

- *American law*: the legal literature of the United States and of the thirteen British colonies that formed the original United States (with apologies to those who justifiably insist that "America" is the name of a continent, not a nation).

- *Ancient law*: the legal literatures of ancient Greece and Mesopotamia.

- *Bibliographies*: both a primary heading and a subheading for systematic listings and descriptions of works of a specific author, subject area, or country. Some auction catalogs, exhibition catalogs, and library catalogs are also indexed as bibliographies.

- *Bibliography*: works on the practice and methodologies of bibliography ("the branch of historical scholarship that examines any aspect of the production, dissemination, and reception of handwritten and printed books as physical objects"[91]) within the field of legal literature, and on its practitioners.

- *Book and manuscript collectors*: individuals of the modern era who have built historical collections of law books and manuscripts, as opposed to private libraries built to support law practice.

- *Dissertations*: brief essays on specific legal topics submitted for doctoral degrees in law from universities in northern Europe (predominantly German and Dutch) in the 16th-19th centuries. In sheer numbers they form the largest genre of legal literature.

- *English law – Civil law*: the legal literature of the English admiralty and ecclesiastical courts, based on Roman and canon law instead of English common law.

- *English law – Readings*: lectures on English statutes, delivered to students at the Inns of Court, which circulated as a form of treatise literature from the 15th century until their demise in the 17th century; a genre unique to English law.

- *European law*: the shared legal literature of continental Europe, including the *ius commune*, the amalgam of canon law, Roman law, and feudal law that was taught predominantly in European and Scottish universities from the Middle Ages through the 18th century.[92] It does not refer to European Union law.

---

[91] G. Thomas Tanselle, "Bibliography Defined," https://bibsocamer.org/about-us/bibliography-defined/.

[92] See Peter Stein, "The Ius Commune and its Demise" (no. 870), at 161.

- *Handbooks and manuals*: procedure manuals, practice guides, justice of the peace manuals, form books, etc.

- *History of the book*: histories of general patterns in the production and consumption of law books.[93]

- *Indian law*: legal literature of the Indian subcontinent.

- *Institutional works*: systematic, concise overviews of a legal system, usually modeled on Justinian's *Institutes*.

- *Latin American law*: the legal literature that Spain and Portugal applied in their New World colonies, along with the legal literature of post-independence Latin America in general.

- *Libraries, private*: the working libraries created and owned by lawyers, judges, law professors, and other legal professionals.

- *Libraries, professional*: libraries of courts, bar associations, the Inns of Court in London, and other legal institutions.

- *Libraries, public*: libraries serving the general public.

- *Library catalogs*: comprehensive listings of a specific library's contents.

- *Manuscript studies*: studies of legal literature produced and disseminated in manuscript, as opposed to print.

- *Medieval law*: works on legal literature from the seventh century up to the advent of printing in 1455.

- *Native American law*: legal literature of the indigenous peoples of the Americas.

---

[93] See Claire M. L. Bourne, "Shakespeare and 'Textual Studies': Evidence, Scale, Periodization and Access," in *The Arden Research Handbook of Shakespeare and Textual Studies* (Lukas Erne, ed.; London: Bloomsbury Publishing, 2021), 21-49, at 22 (defining book history as "broadly conceived to account for the historical production and reception of textual objects); Robert Darnton, "What is the History of Books?", *Daedalus* 111, no. 3 (1982): 65-83, at 66 ("The new book historians ... tried to uncover the general pattern of book production and consumption over long stretches of time").

- *Paratexts*: materials associated with, but distinct from, the main body of a text, such as prefaces, glosses, indexes, and epigraphs.

- *Scandinavia, Scandinavian law:* the legal literature of Denmark, Iceland, Sweden, and Norway (most of the items indexed as "Scandinavian law" deal with the legal literature of medieval Iceland).

- *Textbooks*: literature aimed specifically at law students, including the casebooks of U.S. law schools.

Index to the Checklist

430, 431, 437, 452, 509,
619, 702, 707, 708, 709,
711, 712, 713, 759, 772,
786, 809, 881, 911, 913,
922, 931, 949, 993
American law – Handbooks
and manuals, 79, 89,
108, 131, 177, 196, 260,
416, 435, 445, 750, 834,
924
American law – Illinois, 563
American law – Institutional
works, 371, 426, 446,
550, 760
American law – Kansas, 624
American law – Kentucky,
272, 632, 633, 635, 750
American law – Law reform,
328
American law – Legal re-
search, 46, 366
American law – Louisiana,
86, 87, 92, 163, 164,
165, 166, 180, 208, 246,
327, 508, 509, 702, 707,
708, 709, 711, 712, 713,
749, 759, 772, 839, 913,
931, 993
American law – Massachu-
setts, 195, 219, 863
American law – New Hamp-
shire, 811
American law – New Mexi-
co, 625
American law – New York,
312, 344, 381
American law – North Carolina, 180, 676

American law – Pennsylva-
nia, 131, 332, 333, 334,
335, 336, 337, 338, 339,
340
American law – Periodicals,
91, 111, 141, 188, 247,
249, 253, 310, 311, 336,
337, 340, 366, 374, 391,
423, 436, 519, 644, 645,
832, 833, 837, 894, 924
American law – Popular
works, 67, 182, 190,
202, 257, 376, 425, 429,
449, 608, 609, 610, 611,
851, 945
American law – Pre-Inde-
pendence, 5, 79, 81, 84,
85, 89, 90, 130, 131,
132, 133, 138, 139, 140,
147, 195, 200, 237, 491,
501, 666, 699, 717, 791,
888, 896, 924, 936, 982,
983, 984
American law – Statutes, 55,
92, 145, 274, 304, 316,
332, 344, 361, 366, 519,
713, 750, 811, 863, 883,
889, 913, 924
American law – Texas, 14,
101, 397, 718, 719, 720,
772, 949, 966
American law – Textbooks,
46, 322, 494, 560, 566,
599, 676, 716, 838, 940
American law – Treatises,
16, 86, 170, 241, 295,
312, 321, 466, 467, 491,

Czech law – Medieval, 538

Dalton, Michael (died
1648?), 617

Damhoudere, Joost de
(1507-1581), 488, 646

Dane, Nathan (1752-1835),
500

Davies, John, Sir (1569-
1626), 117

Dictionaries – American law,
262, 396, 612, 628, 631,
712, 992

Dictionaries – English law,
34, 95, 203, 233, 262,
268, 548, 612, 628, 631,
803, 804, 853, 946, 988

Dictionaries – European law,
712

Dictionaries – German law,
535

Dictionaries – Roman law,
262, 535

Digital media – American
law, 75, 76, 77, 124,
240, 242, 274, 400, 403,
517, 812

Dissertations – Germany,
516, 815, 816

Domestic relations, 882

Duck, Arthur, Sir (1580-
1648), 217

Dutch law, 299, 317, 347,
687, 694, 846, 919, 959,
960

Dutch law – Bibliographies,
72, 318, 787

Dutch law – Institutional
works, 920, 973

Dutch law – Medieval, 123

English law, 30, 31, 32, 35,
37, 38, 41, 45, 47, 63,
84, 85, 150, 157, 231,
256, 261, 330, 347, 379,
386, 395, 406, 414, 415,
422, 456, 457, 459, 460,
476, 490, 502, 529, 536,
540, 554, 556, 567, 569,
590, 604, 677, 734, 736,
743, 797, 798, 808, 814,
854, 856, 967, 969, 971,
972, 976

English law – Abridgments
and digests, 98, 99, 232,
233, 268, 388, 455, 603,
803, 804, 824, 897, 906,
974

English law – Bibliogra-
phies, 2, 3, 58, 94, 138,
149, 233, 268, 306, 354,
355, 501, 547, 565, 602,
603, 605, 882, 892, 893,
898, 910

English law – Case reports,
1, 19, 21, 23, 24, 25,
26, 27, 28, 40, 100, 114,
115, 121, 126, 135, 136,
137, 142, 143, 148, 149,
186, 187, 189, 248, 259,
267, 365, 380, 412, 458,
471, 472, 473, 475, 479,
480, 485, 486, 575, 588,
602, 647, 666, 670, 671,
673, 674, 675, 722, 735,

790, 814, 858, 868, 953, 954, 956

Libraries, private – France, 410

Libraries, private – Ireland, 413, 677

Libraries, private – Italy, 51, 175, 597, 692, 705

Libraries, private – Latin America, 245

Libraries, private – Netherlands, 643, 761, 916, 917

Libraries, private – Scotland, 53, 54, 525

Libraries, private – South Africa, 849

Libraries, private – United States, 81, 82, 133, 147, 152, 192, 208, 237, 246, 263, 323, 345, 349, 350, 351, 405, 409, 424, 434, 440, 442, 451, 452, 453, 469, 501, 509, 515, 624, 626, 630, 634, 712, 825, 826, 848, 872, 903, 904, 924, 982, 983, 984

Libraries, professional – Australia, 775

Libraries, professional – Brazil, 779

Libraries, professional – England, 35, 102, 808

Libraries, professional – Ireland, 530, 677

Libraries, professional – Netherlands, 850, 960

Libraries, professional – Portugal, 779

Libraries, professional – Scotland, 525

Libraries, professional – South Africa, 849

Libraries, professional – United States, 68, 69, 103, 104, 129, 167, 185, 287, 288, 289, 360, 451, 468, 552, 624, 630, 821, 848, 896, 900, 924, 949

Libraries, public – United States, 352, 451, 552, 554, 558, 630, 721

Library catalogs – England, 37, 49, 407, 952, 953

Library catalogs – France, 410, 692

Library catalogs – Germany, 689, 690

Library catalogs – Italy, 696

Library catalogs – United States, 206, 349, 350, 351, 352, 440, 442, 452, 515, 594, 634, 825, 826, 900, 936, 949, 982, 983

Linden, Joannes van der (1756-1835), 920

Littleton, Edward (1589-1645), 20

Littleton, Thomas, Sir (died 1481), 422, 565

Livermore, Samuel (1786-1833), 664

Livingston, Edward (1764-1836), 422

Livingston, John (active 1840s-1870s), 433, 871

Checklist of English-Language Publications on the History of Legal Literature, 1921-2022

1. Abbott, L. W. *Law Reporting in England 1485-1585.* London: Athlone Press, 1973.

2. Adams, J. N., & G. Averley. *A Bibliography of Eighteenth Century Legal Literature: A Subject and Author Catalogue of Law Treatises and All Law Related Literature Held in the Main Legal Collections in England.* Newcastle upon Tyne: Avero (Eighteenth-Century) Publications, 1982.

3. Adams, J. N., & M. J. Davies. *A Bibliography of Nineteenth Century Legal Literature: An Author and Subject Catalogue of Law Treatises and All Law Related Literature Held in the Legal Collections of the Inns of Court in England, the British Copyright Libraries, Harvard University Library and the Library of Congress.* 3 vols. Newcastle upon Tyne: Avero Publications & Chadwyck-Healey, 1992-1996.

4. Alexandrowicz, Piotr, & Maria Kola. "*Differentiae iuris civilis et canonici*: The Methodological Premises of an Early Modern German Legal Genre." *Glossae: European Journal of Legal History* 18 (2021): 171-202.

5. American Art Association. *Illustrated Catalogue of Acts and Laws of the Colony and State of New York and of the Other Original Colonies and States: Constituting the Collection Made by Hon. Russell Benedict, Justice of the Supreme Court of New York.* New York: American Art Association, 1922. Reprinted: Union, NJ: Lawbook Exchange, 1998.

6. Anand, R. P. "The Influence of History on the Literature of International Law." In *The Structure and Process of International Law: Essays in Legal Philosophy, Doctrine, and Theory* (Ronald St. J. Macdonald & Douglas M. Johnston, eds.; The Hague: Martinus Nijhoff, 1983), 341-380.

7. Andersen, Per. "From Oral to Written Legal Culture: When Access to the Law is Depersonalized." In *Honos alit artes: studi per il settantesimo compleanno di Mario Ascheri* (4 vols.; Paola Maffei & Gian Maria Varanini, eds.; Firenze: Firenze University Press, 2014), 3:315-324.

8. Andersen, Per. "The Power of the Law: Danish Legal Manuscripts, Legal Culture and the Power of the Book." In *The Power of the Book: Medial Approaches to Medieval Nordic Legal Manuscripts* (Lena Rohrbach, ed.; Berlin: Nordeuropa-Institut der Humboldt-Universität, 2014), 55-74.

9. Anderson, Robert B. "The Harvard Law School Library Under Langdell and Arnold." *Harvard Library Notes* 29 (Mar. 1939): 281-289.

10. Ascheri, Mario. "The Formation of the 'Consilia' Collection of Bartolus of Saxoferrato and Some of His Autographs." In *The Two Laws: Studies in Medieval History Dedicated to Stephan Kuttner* (Laurent Mayali & Stephanie A.J. Tibbets, eds.; Washington: The Catholic University of America, 1990), 188-201.

11. Ascheri, Mario. "Statutory Law of Italian Cities from Middle Ages to Early Modern." In *Von der Ordnung zur Norm: Statuten in Mittelalter und Früher Neuzeit* (Gisela Drossbach, ed.; Paderborn: Ferdinand Schöningh, 2010), 201-216.

12. Ascheri, Mario, & Paola Maffei. "Juridical Late Medieval Paratexts and the Growth of European Jurisprudence." In *Inscribing Knowledge in the Medieval Book: The Power*

of Paratexts (Rosalind Brown-Grant *et al.*, eds.; Berlin: De Gruyter, 2019), 21-45.

13. Aumann, Francis R. "American Law Reports: Yesterday and Today." *Ohio State University Law Journal* 4, no. 3 (June 1938): 331-345.

14. Baade, Hans W. "Rare Books and Rare Lawyers in Eighteenth-Century Texas." In *Collecting and Managing Rare Law Books: Papers Presented at a Conference Celebrating the Dedication of the New Tarlton Law Library, the University of Texas at Austin School of Law, January 7 & 8, 1981* (Roy M. Mersky & Stanley Ferguson, eds.; Dobbs Ferry, NY: Oceana Publications, 1981), 293-315.

15. Bair, Lorne, Hélène Golay, & Michael Widener. *Free Tom Mooney! An Exhibition of the Yale Law Library's Tom Mooney Collection on the Centennial of Mooney's Frame-up*. New Haven: Lillian Goldman Law Library, Yale Law School, 2016.

16. Baker, G. Blaine. "Story'd Paradigms for the Nineteenth-Century Display of Anglo-American Legal Doctrine." In *Law Books in Action: Essays on the Anglo-American Legal Treatise* (Angela Fernandez & Markus D. Dubber, eds.; Oxford: Hart Publishing, 2012), 82-107.

17. Baker, G. Blaine. "Popularizing the Rule of Law: Sheldon Amos and the International Scientific Series, 1874 to 1909." *Journal of Legal History* 33, no. 2 (Aug. 2012): 151-184.

18. Baker, G. Blaine. "Musings and Silences of Chief Justice William Osgoode: Digest Marginalia about the Reception of Imperial Law." *Osgoode Hall Law Journal* 54, no. 3 (Spring 2017): 741-776.

19. Baker, John H. "Coke's Note-Books and the Sources of his Reports." *Cambridge Law Journal* 30, no. 1 (Apr. 1972): 59-86.

84

20. Baker, John H. "The Newe Littleton." *Cambridge Law Journal* 33, no. 1 (Apr. 1974): 145-155. Reprinted: John H. Baker, *Collected Papers on English Legal History* (Cambridge, UK: Cambridge University Press, 2013), 2:768-781.

21. Baker, John H. "Case-Law: Reports and Records." In *Englische und Kontinentale Rechtsgeschichte: Ein Forschungsprojekt* (H. Coing & K. W. Nörr, eds.; Berlin: Duncker & Humblot, 1985), 49-55.

22. Baker, John H. "Dr. Thomas Fastolf and the History of Law Reporting." *Cambridge Law Journal* 45, no. 1 (Mar. 1986): 84-96.

23. Baker, John H. "Early Tudor Reports and the Plea Rolls." *Cambrian Law Review* 18 (1987): 25-33.

24. Baker, John H. "Records, Reports and the Origins of Case-Law in England." In *Judicial Records, Law Reports, and the Growth of Case Law* (John H. Baker, ed.; Berlin: Duncker & Humblot, 1989), 15-46.

25. Baker, John H. "John Bryt's Reports (1410-1411) and the Year Books of Henry IV." *Cambridge Law Journal* 48, no. 1 (Mar. 1989): 98-114.

26. Baker, John H. "Law Reports and English Legal History: The Editorial Problem." In *Studi in Memoria di Gino Gorla* (L. Moccia, ed.; Milan: Giuffré, 1994), 155-171.

27. Baker, John H. "Some Early Newgate Reports (1315-28)." In *Law Reporting in Britain* (Chantal Stebbings, ed.; London: Hambledon Press, 1995), 35-53.

28. Baker, John H. "The Common-Law Courts of Medieval England: Year Books and Plea Rolls." In *Case Law in the Making: The Techniques and Methods of Judicial Records and Law Reports* (Alain A. Wijffels, ed.; Berlin: Duncker & Humblot, 1997), 1:39-54.

29. Baker, John H. *Monuments of Endlesse Labours: English Canonists and Their Work, 1300-1900.* London: Hambledon Press, 1998.

30. Baker, John H. "The Books of the Common Law." In *The Cambridge History of the Book in Britain, Volume III, 1400-1557* (Cambridge: Cambridge University Press, 1998), 411-432.

31. Baker, John H. "English Law Books and Legal Publishing." In *The Cambridge History of the Book in Britain, Volume IV, 1557-1696* (Cambridge: Cambridge University Press, 1998), 474-503.

32. Baker, John H. *The Common Law Tradition: Lawyers, Books, and the Law*. London: Hambledon Press, 2000.

33. Baker, John H. *Readers and Readings in the Inns of Court and Chancery*. London: Selden Society, 2001.

34. Baker, John H. "John Rastell and the Terms of the Law." In *Language and the Law: Proceedings of a Conference, December 6-8, 2001, Tarlton Law Library, The University of Texas at Austin* (Marlyn Robinson, ed.; Buffalo, N.Y.: William S. Hein & Co., 2003), 15-30. Reprinted: John H. Baker, *Collected Papers on English Legal History* (Cambridge, UK: Cambridge University Press, 2013), 2:709-721.

35. Baker, John H. "Common Lawyers and the Inns of Court." In *Libraries in Britain and Ireland: Volume 1, to 1640* (E. Leedham-Green & T. Webber, eds.; Cambridge, UK: Cambridge University Press, 2006), 448-460. Reprinted: "Common Lawyers' Libraries 1450-1650," in John H. Baker, *Collected Papers on English Legal History* (Cambridge, UK: Cambridge University Press, 2013), 2:697-708.

36. Baker, John H. "Books of Entries." *Irish Jurist* 41 (2006): 1-19. Reprinted: John H. Baker, *Collected Papers on English Legal History* (Cambridge, UK: Cambridge University Press, 2013), 2:670-690.

37. Baker, John H., & Anthony Taussig. *A Catalogue of the Legal Manuscripts of Anthony Taussig*. London: Selden Society, 2007.

38. Baker, John H. *English Legal Manuscripts Formerly in the Collection of Sir Thomas Phillipps*. London: Selden Society, 2008.

39. Baker, John H. *The Reinvention of Magna Carta 1216-1616*. Cambridge, UK: Cambridge University Press, 2017.

40. Baker, John H. "Law Reporting in England 1550-1650." *International Journal of Legal Information* 45, no. 3 (Nov. 2017): 209-218.

41. Baker, John H. "Legal Literature." In John H. Baker, *An Introduction to English Legal History* (5th ed.; Oxford, UK: Oxford University Press, 2019), 185-205.

42. Ballone, Angela. "Contextualising the papal censure of the *Disputationes de Indiarum Iure* (1642): The *consultores* of the Congregation of the Index." *Colonial Latin American Review* 27, no. 1 (2018): 73-113.

43. Ballone, Angela. "Foreign Law Without Borders in the Early Vast America: Spanish Legal Literature in 18th Century North America." *Tijdschrift voor Rechtsgeschiedenis / Legal History Review* 89, nos. 1-2 (July 2021): 212-241.

44. Ballone, Angela. "Foreign Law Without Borders in the Early Vast America: Spanish Legal Literature in 19th Century North America." *Clio@Themis* 21 (2021). https://doi.org/10.35562/cliothemis.1946

45. Baloch, Tariq. "Law Booksellers and Printers as Agents of Unchange." *Cambridge Law Journal* 66, no. 2 (July 2007): 385-421.

46. Barkan, Steven M. "On Describing Legal Research." *Michigan Law Review* 80, no. 4 (Mar. 1982): 925-941. [Review essay of J. Myron Jacobstein & Roy M. Mersky, *Fundamentals of Legal Research* (Mineola, NY: Foundation Press, 1981).]

47. Barker, Nicolas. "The Law in Manuscript." *The Book Collector* 57, no. 3 (Autumn 2008): 335-348. [Review

essay of no. 37: John H. Baker & Anthony Taussig, *A Catalogue of the Legal Manuscripts of Anthony Taussig* (London: Selden Society, 2007).]

48. Barnes, Thomas Garden. *Shaping the Common Law: From Glanvill to Hale, 1188-1688.* Stanford, CA: Stanford University Press, 2008.

49. Barratt, Dorothy M. "The Library of John Selden and its Later History." With Appendices A-C. *Bodleian Library Record* 3, no. 31 (Mar. 1951): 128-142; 3, no. 32 (Aug. 1951): 208-213; 3, no. 33 (Dec. 1951): 256-274.

50. Barrêtto de Almeida Costa, Arthur. "The Tropical Fado that Wanted to Become a European Samba: The Cosmopolitan Structure of Brazilian Administrative Law Investigated with Bibliometric Data (1859-1930)." *Forum Historiae Iuris* (2021). https://forhistiur.net/landingpage/375/

51. Bartocci, Andrea. "John of Capestrano and His Itinerant Library: Some Observations on His Legal Books." *Rivista Internazionale di Diritto Comune* 31 (2020): 321-328.

52. Barton, J. L. "The Authorship of Bracton: Again." *Journal of Legal History* 30, no. 2 (Aug. 2009): 117-174.

53. Baston, Karen. *Charles Areskine's Library: Lawyers and Their Books at the Dawn of the Scottish Enlightenment.* Leiden: Brill, 2016.

54. Baston, Karen G. "Humanist Books and Lawyers' Libraries in Early Eighteenth Century Scotland: Charles Areskine of Alva's Library." In *Reassessing Legal Humanism and Its Claims: Petere Fontes?* (Paul J. du Plessis & John W. Cairns, eds.; Edinburgh: Edinburgh University Press, 2016), 348-376.

55. Bates, Albert C. "Early Connecticut Laws." *Papers of the Bibliographical Society of America* 40, no. 2 (June 1946): 151-158.

56. Baum, Marsha L., & Christian G. Fritz. "American Constitution-Making: The Neglected State Constitutional Sources." *Hastings Constitutional Law Quarterly* 27, no. 2 (Winter 2000): 199-242.

57. Beale, Joseph H. "The Early English Statutes." *Harvard Law Review* 35, no. 5 (Mar. 1922): 519-538.

58. Beale, Joseph H. *Bibliography of Early English Law Books.* Cambridge, MA: Harvard University Press, 1926. [With] Anderson, Robert B. *A Supplement to Beale's Bibliography of Early English Law Books.* Cambridge, MA: Harvard University Press, 1943. Reprinted: Buffalo, NY: Dennis, 1966.

59. Beck Varela, Laura. "The Diffusion of Law Books in Early Modern Europe: A Methodological Approach." In *Spatial and Temporal Dimensions for Legal History: Research Experiences and Itineraries* (M. Meccarelli & J. Solla, eds.; Frankfurt am Main: Max Planck Institute for European Legal History, 2016), 195-239.

60. Beck Varela, Laura. "Translating Law for Women? The *Institutes du droit civil pour les dames* in Eighteenth-Century Helmstedt." *Rechtsgeschichte - Legal History (Rg)* 24 (2016): 171-189.

61. Beck Varela, Laura. "Authorship in Early Modern Jurisprudence: Paul Voet (1619-1667) on *auctor* and *editor*." *Quaerendo* 47, nos. 3-4 (Dec. 2017): 252-277.

62. Beck, Karen S., Mary Sarah Bilder, & Ann McDonald. *Collectors on Collecting.* Boston: Boston College Law Library, 2002.

63. Beck, Karen S. *Kitty Preyer and Her Books.* Boston: Boston College Law Library, 2006.

64. Beck, Karen S. *The Michael H. Hoeflich Collection of Roman Law Books – Spring 2011: An Illustrated Guide to the Exhibit.* Boston: Boston College Law Library, 2011.

65. Beckerman, John S. "Law-Writing and Law-Teaching: Treatise Evidence of the Formal Teaching of English Law in the Late Thirteenth Century." In *Learning the Law: Teaching and the Transmission of Law in England, 1150-1900* (Jonathan Bush & Alain A. Wijffels, eds.; London: Hambledon Press, 1999), 33-50.

66. Beech, Beatrice Hibbard. "Charlotte Guillard: A Sixteenth-Century Business Woman." *Renaissance Quarterly* 36, no. 3 (Autumn 1983): 345-367.

67. Behrens, Jennifer L. "Beyond 'The Annals of Murder': The Life and Works of Thomas M. McDade." *Law Library Journal* 111, no. 3 (Summer 2019): 281-306.

68. Bellefontaine, Edgar J. "The Social Law Library: 175 Years of Service to the Bench and Bar of Massachusetts." *Boston Bar Journal* (Nov. 1980): 5-23.

69. Bellefontaine, Edgar J., & James A. Brink. "The History of the Social Law Library." In *Law Librarianship: Historical Perspectives* (Laura N. Gasaway & Michael G. Chiorazzi, eds.; Littleton, CO: F. B. Rothman, 1996), 111-161.

70. Belniak, Theodora. "The History of the American Bar Association Accreditation Standards for Academic Law Libraries." *Law Library Journal* 106, no. 2 (Spring 2014): 151-173.

71. Bennett, J. M., & N. J. Haxton. "Law Reporting and Law Authoring." In *No Mere Mouthpiece: Servants of All, Yet of None.* (G. Lindsay, ed.; Sydney, Butterworths, 2002).

72. Bergh, G. C. J. J. van den. *The Life and Work of Gerard Noodt, 1647-1725: Dutch Legal Scholarship between Humanism and Enlightenment.* New York: Oxford University Press, 1988.

73. Berkowitz, David S. "Projects for a Biography and Edition of John Selden's Works, 1654-1766." *Quaerendo* 4, no. 3 (Jan. 1974): 247-257.

74. Berring, Robert C. "Legal Research and Legal Concepts: Where Form Molds Substance." *California Law Review* 75, no. 1 (Jan. 1987): 15-28.

75. Berring, Robert C. "Chaos, Cyberspace and Tradition: Legal Information Transmogrified." *Berkeley Technology Law Journal* 12, no. 1 (1997): 189-212.

76. Berring, Robert C. "Legal Research and the World of Thinkable Thoughts." *Journal of Appellate Practice and Process* 2, no. 2 (Summer 2000): 305-318.

77. Berring, Robert C. "Legal Information and the Search for Cognitive Authority." *California Law Review* 88, no. 6 (Dec. 2000): 1673-1708.

78. Berring, Robert C. "The Ultimate Oldie but Goodie: William Blackstone's *Commentaries on the Law of England*." *Journal of Law* 4, no. 2 (2014): 189-194.

79. Berry, Nathaniel J. "Justice of the Peace Manuals in Virginia before 1800." *Journal of Southern Legal History* 26 (2018): 315-350.

80. Bessler, John D. "The Marquis Beccaria: An Italian Penal Reformer's Meteoric Rise in the British Isles in the Transatlantic Republic of Letters." *Diciottesimo Secolo* 4 (2019): 107-120. https://doi.org/10.13128/ds-25443

81. Bilder, Mary Sarah. "The Lost Lawyers: Early American Legal Literates and Transatlantic Legal Culture." *Yale Journal of Law & the Humanities* 11, no. 1 (Winter 1999): 47-117.

82. Bilder, Mary Sarah, & Laurel Davis. *Robert Morris: Lawyer and Activist.* Boston: Boston College Law Library, 2017.

83. Billings, Carol D. "Sources for the Study of the Constitutional Era: A Bibliographical and Historiographical Essay." *Law Library Journal* 81, no. 1 (Winter 1989): 47-67.

84. Billings, Warren M. "English Legal Literature as a Source of Law and Practice in Seventeenth-Century

Virginia." *Virginia Magazine of History and Biography* 87 (1979): 403-417. Reprinted: Warren M. Billings, *Magistrates and Pioneers: Essays in the History of American Law* (Clark, NJ: Lawbook Exchange, 2011), 71-92; *"Esteemed bookes of lawe" and the Legal Culture of Early Virginia* (Warren M. Billings & Brent Tarter, eds.; Charlottesville: University of Virginia Press, 2017), 11-26.

85. Billings, Warren M. "Justices, Books, Laws, and Courts in Seventeenth-Century Virginia." *Law Library Journal* 85, no. 2 (Spring 1993): 277-296.

86. Billings, Warren M. "A Neglected Treatise: Lewis Kerr's *Exposition* and the Making of Criminal Law in Louisiana." *Louisiana History* 38, no. 3 (Summer 1997): 261-286. Reprinted: Warren M. Billings, *Magistrates and Pioneers: Essays in the History of American Law.* Clark, NJ: Lawbook Exchange, 2011.

87. Billings, Warren M. "A Course of Legal Studies: Books That Shaped Louisiana Law." In *A Law Unto Itself? Essays in the New Louisiana Legal History* (Warren M. Billings & Mark F. Fernandez, eds.; Baton Rouge: Louisiana State University Press, 2001), 25-39.

88. Billings, Warren M. *An Accidental Collector: The Making of an Historian's Law Library.* Austin, TX: Jamail Center for Legal Research, The University of Texas at Austin, 2013.

89. Billings, Warren M. "A Virginia Original: George Webb's *Office and Authority of a Justice of Peace.*" In *"Esteemed bookes of lawe" and the Legal Culture of Early Virginia* (Warren M. Billings & Brent Tarter, eds.; Charlottesville: University of Virginia Press, 2017), 157-177.

90. Billings, Warren M. "William Gooch and Law Books in Colonial Virginia." *Unbound: A Review of Legal History and Rare Books* 12, no. 1 (Spring/Summer 2020): 5-16.

https://www.aallnet.org/lhrbsis/resources-publications/unbound/

91. Billings, Warren M. "Gustavus Schmidt and The Louisiana Law Journal." *Unbound: A Review of Legal History and Rare Books* 12, no. 2 (Winter/Spring 2021): 6-18. https://www.aallnet.org/lhrbsis/resources-publications/unbound/

92. Billings, Warren M. "James Morgan Bradford and Print Culture in Early Louisiana." *Unbound: A Review of Legal History and Rare Books* 13, no. 1 (Summer 2022): 5-23. https://www.aallnet.org/lhrbsis/resources-publications/unbound/

93. Biscardi, Francine. "The Historical Development of the Law Concerning Judicial Report Publication." *Law Library Journal* 85, no. 3 (Summer 1993): 531-544.

94. Bland, D. S. *A Bibliography of the Inns of Court and Chancery*. London: Selden Society, 1965.

95. Bland, D. S. "Some Notes on the Evolution of the Legal Dictionary." *Journal of Legal History* 1, no. 1 (May 1980): 75-84.

96. Bochove, Thomas Ernst van. *To Date and Not to Date: On the Date and Status of Byzantine Law Books*. Groningen: E. Forsten, 1996.

97. Boersma, Frederick Lister. "Fitzherbert's *Natura Brevium*: A Bibliographic Survey." *Law Library Journal* 71, no. 2 (May 1978): 257-265.

98. Boersma, Frederick Lister. "Sir Antony Fitzherbert: A Biographical Sketch and Short Bibliography." *Law Library Journal* 71, no. 3 (Aug. 1978): 387-400.

99. Boersma, Frederick Lister. *An Introduction to Fitzherbert's Abridgement*. Abingdon, UK: Professional Books, 1981.

100. Bolland, William Craddock. *A Manual of Year Book Studies*. Cambridge, UK: University Press, 1925.

alization...

101. Boner, Marian O. *A Reference Guide to Texas Law and Legal History: Sources and Documentation*. Austin, TX: University of Texas Press, 1976.

102. Bonhams & Brooks. *Law Books: Sold by Order of the Birmingham Law Society*. London: Bonhams & Brooks, 2001.

103. Bonhams. *Law Books: Property of LA Law Library, Part One*. London: Bonhams, 2014.

104. Bonhams. *Law Books: Property of LA Law Library, Part Two*. Oxford, UK: Bonhams, 2014.

105. Boorstin, Daniel J. *The Mysterious Science of the Law: An Essay on Blackstone's Commentaries*. Boston: Beacon Press, 1958.

106. Boorstin, Daniel J. "Printing and the Constitution." In *The Republic of Letters: Librarian of Congress Daniel J. Boorstin on Books, Reading, and Libraries, 1975-1987* (John Y. Cole, ed.; Washington, D.C.: Library of Congress, 1989), 97-107.

107. Boulhosa, Patricia Pires. "Layout and the Structure of the Text in Kongungsbók." In *The Power of the Book: Medial Approaches to Medieval Nordic Legal Manuscripts* (Lena Rohrbach, ed.; Berlin: Nordeuropa-Institut der Humboldt-Universität, 2014), 75-97.

108. Boyer, Larry M. "The Justice of the Peace in England and America from 1506 to 1776: A Bibliographic History." *Quarterly Journal of the Library of Congress* 34, no. 4 (Oct. 1977): 315-326.

109. Bragagnolo, Manuela. "Managing Legal Knowledge in Early Modern Times: Martín de Azpilcueta's *Manual for Confessors* and the Phenomenon of Epitomisation." In *Knowledge of the* Pragmatici: *Legal and Moral Theological Literature and the Formation of Early Modern Ibero-America* (Thomas Duve & Otto Danwerth, eds.; Leiden: Brill Nijhoff, 2020), 187-242.

110. Bragagnolo, Manuela. "Books in Motion and Normative Knowledge Production in the Early Modern Iberian Worlds: An Introduction." *Rechtsgeschichte - Legal History (Rg)* 29 (2021): 92-98.

111. Brainerd, Marion. "Historical Sketch of American Legal Periodicals." *Law Library Journal* 14, no. 3 (Oct. 1921): 63-69.

112. Brand, Paul. "*Hengham Magna*: A Thirteenth Century English Common Law Treatise and Its Composition." *Irish Jurist* 11, no. 1 (Summer 1976): 147-169.

113. Brand, Paul. "Ireland and the Literature of the Early Common Law." *Irish Jurist* 16, no. 1 (Summer 1981): 95-113.

114. Brand, Paul. "The Beginnings of English Law Reporting." In *Law Reporting in Britain* (Chantal Stebbings, ed.; London: Hambledon Press, 1995), 1-14.

115. Brand, Paul. *Observing and Recording the Medieval Bar and Bench at Work: The Origins of Law Reporting in England: Selden Society Lecture Delivered in the Old Hall of Lincoln's Inn, July 6th, 1998*. London: Selden Society, 1999.

116. Brand, Paul. "Legal Education in England before the Inns of Court." In *Learning the Law: Teaching and the Transmission of Law in England, 1150-1900* (Jonathan Bush & Alain A. Wijffels, eds.; London: Hambledon Press, 1999), 51-84.

117. Brand, Paul. "Sir John Davies: Law Reporter or Self-Publicist?" *Irish Jurist* 43 (2008): 1-20.

118. Brand, Paul. "The Date and Authorship of *Bracton*: A Response." *Journal of Legal History* 31, no. 3 (Dec. 2010): 217-244.

119. Brand, Paul. "The First Century of Magna Carta: The Diffusion of Texts and Knowledge of the Charter." *William & Mary Bill of Rights Journal* 25, no. 2 (Dec. 2016): 437-454.

120. Breatnach, Liam. *A Companion to the Corpus Iuris Hibernici.* Dublin: Dublin Institute for Advanced Studies, 2005.

121. Breem, Wallace. "The Law Journal Reports." *Law Librarian* 16, no. 3 (Dec. 1985): 114-116.

122. Breem, Wallace, & Sally Phillips. *Bibliography of Commonwealth Law Reports.* London & New York: Mansell, 1991.

123. Bremmer, Rolf H., Jr. "Codifying the Law: Frisian Legal Manuscripts around 1300." In *Vernacular Manuscript Culture 1000-1500* (Erik Kwakkel, ed.; Leiden: Leiden University Press, 2018), 143-185.

124. Brenner, Susan W. "Of Publication and Precedent: An Inquiry into the Ethnomethodology of Case Reporting in the American Legal System." *DePaul Law Review* 39, no. 3 (Spring 1990): 461-542.

125. Briceland, A. V. "Ephraim Kirby: Pioneer of American Law Reporting, 1789." *American Journal of Legal History* 16, no. 4 (Oct. 1972): 297-319.

126. Bricker, Andrew B. "The Functions of Legal Literature and Case Reporting Before and After Stare Decisis." In *The Oxford Handbook of Law and Humanities* (Simon Stern *et al.*, eds.; New York: Oxford University Press, 2020), 619-638.

127. Brink, Stefan. "Librum legum terre Haelsingie: The Inspection and Approval of Versions of the Law-Book of the Hälsingar." In *The Power of the Book: Medial Approaches to Medieval Nordic Legal Manuscripts* (Lena Rohrbach, ed.; Berlin: Nordeuropa-Institut der Humboldt-Universität, 2014), 157-162.

128. Brito Vieira, Mónica. "Mare Liberum vs. Mare Clausum: Grotius, Freitas, and Selden's Debate on Dominion over the Seas." *Journal of the History of Ideas* 64, no. 3 (July 2003): 361-377.

129. Brock, Christine A. "Law Libraries and Librarians: A Revisionist History; or More Than You Ever Wanted to Know." *Law Library Journal* 67, no. 3 (Aug. 1974): 325-361. Reprinted: *Law Librarianship: Historical Perspectives* (Laura N. Gasaway & Michael G. Chiorazzi, eds.; Littleton, CO: F. B. Rothman, 1996), 597-633.

130. Bronner, Edwin B. "First Printing of Magna Carta in America, 1687." *American Journal of Legal History* 7, no. 3 (July 1963): 189-199.

131. Brophy, Alfred L. "'Ingenium est Fateri per quos profeceris': Francis Daniel Pastorius' *Young Country Clerk's Collection* and Anglo-American Legal Literature, 1682-1716." *University of Chicago Law School Roundtable* 3, no. 2 (1996): 637-734.

132. Brophy, Alfred L. "The Law Book in Colonial America." *Buffalo Law Review* 51, no. 4 (Fall 2003): 1119-1143. [Review essay of David Hall & Hugh Amory, eds., *A History of the Book in America: The Colonial Book in the Atlantic World* (Cambridge, U.K.: Cambridge University Press, 1999).]

133. Brown, Bennie. "John Mercer: Merchant, Lawyer, Author, Book Collector." In *"Esteemed bookes of lawe" and the Legal Culture of Early Virginia* (Warren M. Billings & Brent Tarter, eds.; Charlottesville: University of Virginia Press, 2017), 95-112.

134. Browne, Cynthia E. *State Constitutional Conventions from Independence to the Completion of the Present Union, 1776-1959: A Bibliography.* Westport, CT: Greenwood Press, 1973.

135. Bryan, Michael. "Early English Law Reporting." *University of Melbourne Collections* (June 2009), 45-50.

136. Bryan, Michael. "The Modern History of Law Reporting." *University of Melbourne Collections* (Dec. 2012), 32-36.

137. Bryson, William Hamilton. "A Note on Robinson's Brief Collection of ... Courts of Records." *Transactions of the Cambridge Bibliographical Society* 6, no. 3 (1974): 181-187.

138. Bryson, William Hamilton. *Census of Law Books in Colonial Virginia.* Charlottesville, VA: University Press of Virginia, 1978.

139. Bryson, William Hamilton. "Law Reporting and Legal Records in Virginia, 1607-1800." In *Judicial Records, Law Reports, and the Growth of Case Law* (J. H. Baker, ed.; Berlin: Duncker & Humblot, 1989), 319-335.

140. Bryson, William Hamilton. "Virginia Manuscript Law Reports." *Law Library Journal* 82, no. 2 (Spring 1990): 305-311.

141. Bryson, William Hamilton, & J. N. Jorgensen. "Twentieth-Century Virginia Legal Periodicals: A Bibliography and Commentary." *Law Library Journal* 86, no. 3 (Summer 1994): 541-558.

142. Bryson, William Hamilton. "Law Reports in England from 1603 to 1660." In *Law Reporting in Britain* (Chantal Stebbings, ed.; London: Hambledon Press, 1995), 113-122.

143. Bryson, William Hamilton. "Equity Reports and Records in Early-Modern England." In *Case Law in the Making: The Techniques and Methods of Judicial Records and Law Reports* (Alain A. Wijffels, ed.; Berlin: Duncker & Humblot, 1997), 1:69-82.

144. Bryson, William Hamilton. "Virginia Law Reports and Records, 1776-1800." In *Case Law in the Making: The Techniques and Methods of Judicial Records and Law Reports* (Alain A. Wijffels, ed.; Berlin: Duncker & Humblot, 1997), 1:99-108.

145. Bryson, William Hamilton. "The Code of Virginia of 1849." In *Within a Reasonable Time: The History of Due*

98

and Undue Delay in Civil Litigation (C. H. van Rhee, ed.; Berlin: Duncker & Humblot, 2010), 199-214.

146. Bryson, William Hamilton. "Virginia Law Reports." *American Journal of Legal History* 54, no. 2 (2014): 107-120.

147. Bryson, William Hamilton. "Law Books in the Libraries of Colonial Virginians." In *"Esteemed bookes of lawe" and the Legal Culture of Early Virginia* (Warren M. Billings & Brent Tarter, eds.; Charlottesville: University of Virginia Press, 2017), 27-36.

148. Bryson, William Hamilton. "Law Reporting in the Seventeenth Century." In *English Legal History and Its Sources: Essays in Honour of Sir John Baker* (David Ibbetson *et al.*, eds.; Cambridge: Cambridge University Press, 2019), 44-53.

149. Bryson, William Hamilton. *Some English Law Reporters of Seventeenth Century Cases: A Bibliography.* Richmond, VA: W. H. Bryson, 2020.

150. Bühler, Curt F. "Notes on a Pynson Volume." *The Library: Transactions of the Bibliographical Society,* 4th series 18, no. 3 (Dec. 1937): 261-267.

151. Burns, J. H. "The 'Monarchia' of Antonio Roselli (1380-1466): Text, Context and Controversy." In *Proceedings of the Eighth International Congress of Medieval Canon Law: San Diego, University of California at La Jolla, 21-27 August 1988* (Stanley Chodorow, ed.; Città del Vaticano: Biblioteca Apostolica Vaticana, 1992), 321-351.

152. Butler, William E. *Peter Stephen Du Ponceau, Legal Bibliophile.* Austin, TX: Jamail Center for Legal Research, University of Texas at Austin, 2010.

153. Butler, William E., N. V. Hendel, & T. R. Korotkyi. "The Legal Scholarship of P. E. Kazanskii: A Bio-Bibliographical Essay." *Jus Gentium: Journal of International Legal History* 1, no. 1 (Jan. 2016): 141-182.

154. Butler, William E., & Michael Kwon. "Manning's *Commentaries on the Law of Nations.*" *Jus Gentium: Journal of International Legal History* 4, no. 2 (July 2019): 621-632.

155. Butler, William E. *Grotius on War and Peace in English Translation.* Clark, NJ: Talbot Publishing, 2021.

156. Butler, William E. "The English Translators and Publishers of Grotius on War and Peace: 1654-1928." *Jus Gentium: Journal of International Legal History* 6, no. 2 (July 2021): 441-552.

157. Byrom, H. J. "Richard Tottell, His Life and Work." *The Library: Transactions of the Bibliographical Society*, 4th series 8, no. 2 (Sept. 1927): 199-232.

158. Caenegem, R. C. van. "The Holy Books of the Law." In R. C. van Caenegem, *European Law in the Past and the Future: Unity and Diversity over Two Millenia* (Cambridge, UK: Cambridge University Press, 2002), 54-72.

159. Cairns, John W. "Institutional Writings in Scotland Reconsidered." *Journal of Legal History* 4, no. 3 (Dec. 1983): 76-117.

160. Cairns, John W. "Blackstone, an English Institutist: Legal Literature and the Rise of the Nation State." *Oxford Journal of Legal Studies* 4, no. 3 (Winter 1984): 318-360. Reprinted: John W. Cairns, *Law, Lawyers, and Humanism: Selected Essays on the History of Scots Law, Vol 1* (Edinburgh: Edinburgh University Press, 2015), 413-461.

161. Cairns, John W. "The Moveable Text of Mackenzie: Bibliographical Problems for the Scottish Concept of Institutional Writing." In *Critical Studies in Ancient Law, Comparative Law and Legal History: Essays in Honour of Alan Watson* (John W. Cairns & Olivia F. Robinson, eds; Oxford: Hart Publishing 2001), 235-248. Reprinted: John W. Cairns, *Law, Lawyers, and Humanism: Selected*

Essays on the History of Scots Law, Vol 1 (Edinburgh: Edinburgh University Press, 2015), 498-513.

162. Cairns, John W. "Law Books: 1707-1918." In *The Edinburgh History of Scottish Literature: Enlightenment, Britain and Empire (1707-1918)* (Ian Brown, *et al.*, eds.; Edinburgh: Edinburgh University Press, 2006), 191-197.

163. Cairns, John W. "The De la Vergne Volume and the Digest of 1808." *Tulane European & Civil Law Forum* 24, no. 1 (2009): 31-82.

164. Cairns, John W. "Blackstone in the Bayous: Inscribing Slavery in the Louisiana *Digest* of 1808." In *Re-interpreting Blackstone's Commentaries: A Seminal Text in National and International Contexts* (Wilfrid Prest, ed.; Oxford, UK: Hart Publishing, 2014), 73-94.

165. Cairns, John W. "Spanish Law, the *Teatro de la Legislación Universal de España e Indias*, and the Background to the Drafting of the Digest of Orleans of 1808." *Tulane European & Civil Law Forum* 31-32 (2017), 79-120.

166. Cairns, John W. "Introductory Essay to the Translation of the Discurso Preliminar of Pérez y López's *Teatro*." *Journal of Civil Law Studies* 11, no. 2 (2018): 433-464.

167. Cajero, Channa, & Sandra Levin. "Gems from California's Legal History at LA Law Library." *California Legal History* 14 (2019): 273-290.

168. *The Cambridge History of Medieval Canon Law*. Anders Winroth & John C. Wei, eds. Cambridge, UK: Cambridge University Press, 2022.

169. Camille, Michael. "At the Edge of the Law: An Illustrated Register of Writs in the Pierpont Morgan Library." In *England in the Fourteenth Century: Proceedings of the 1991 Harlaxton Symposium* (Nicholas Rogers, ed.; Stamford, UK: Paul Watkins, 1993), 1-14.

170. Campbell, Lyndsay. "Truth and Privilege: Libel Treatises and the Transmission of Legal Norms in the Early

Nineteenth-Century Anglo-American World." In *Law Books in Action: Essays on the Anglo-American Legal Treatise* (Angela Fernandez & Markus D. Dubber, eds.; Oxford: Hart Publishing, 2012), 165-180.

171. Castles, Alex C. *Annotated Bibliography of Printed Materials on Australian Law 1788-1900*. North Ryde, NSW: Law Book Company, 1994.

172. Caswell, Jean, & Ivan Sipkov. *The Coutumes of France in the Library of Congress: An Annotated Bibliography.* Washington, DC: Library of Congress, 1977. Reprinted: Clark, NJ: Lawbook Exchange, 2006.

173. Cavallar, Osvaldo, Susanne Degenring, & Julius Kirshner. *A Grammar of Signs: Bartolo da Sassoferrato's Tract on Insignia and Coats of Arms.* Berkeley: Robbins Collection Publications, School of Law, University of California, 1994.

174. Cavallar, Osvaldo. "River of Law: Bartolus's Tiberiadis (De alluvione)." In *A Renaissance of Conflicts: Visions and Revisions of Law and Society in Italy and Spain* (J.A. Marino & T. Kuehn, eds.; Toronto: Centre for Reformation and Renaissance Studies, 2004), 30-129.

175. Cavallar, Osvaldo, & Julius Kirshner. "'Many Books'." In *Jurists and Jurisprudence in Medieval Italy: Texts and Contexts* (Osvaldo Cavallar & Julius Kirshner, eds.; Toronto: University of Toronto Press, 2020), 150-158.

176. Cazals, Géraldine, Sabrina Michel, & Alain A. Wijffels. "Law Reports of the Parliament of Flanders and their Authority in the Parliament's Practice." In *Authorities in Early Modern Law Courts* (Guido Rossi, ed.; Edinburgh: Edinburgh University Press, 2021), 1-28.

177. Chandler, R. H., Jr., & Michael H. Hoeflich. "Law for Farmers in Nineteenth-Century America." *Law Library Journal* 109, no. 4 (Fall 2017): 673-681.

178. Cheney, C. R. "William Lyndwood's *Provinciale*." *The Jurist* 21, no. 4 (Oct. 1961): 405-434.

179. Cheskis, Joel Howard. "Copyright of Legal Materials: From Wheaton to West - Shaping the Practice of Law in America." *Communications and the Law* 20, no. 3 (1998): 1-38.

180. Chiorazzi, Michael. "Francois-Xavier Martin: Printer, Lawyer, Jurist." *Law Library Journal* 80, no. 1 (Winter 1988): 63-98.

181. Chodorow, Stanley. *Law Libraries and the Formation of the Legal Profession in the Late Middle Ages.* Austin, TX: Jamail Center for Legal Research, the University of Texas at Austin, 2007.

182. Chute, Hillary. "Comics." In *The Oxford Handbook of Law and Humanities* (Simon Stern *et al.*, eds.; New York: Oxford University Press, 2020), 821-839.

183. Clarence Smith, J. A. *Medieval Law Teachers and Writers, Civilian and Canonist.* Ottawa: University of Ottawa Press, 1975.

184. Clark, David S. "Nation Building and Law Collections: The Remarkable Development of Comparative Law Libraries in the United States." *Law Library Journal* 109, no. 4 (Fall 2017): 499-556.

185. Clarke, Oscar D. "The Library of the Supreme Court of the United States." *Law Library Journal* 31, no. 3 (May 1938): 89-102.

186. Clinch, Peter. "The Establishment v. Butterworths: New Light on a Little Known Chapter in the History of English Law Reporting." *Anglo-American Law Review* 19, no. 3 (1990): 209-238.

187. Clinch, Peter. "'To Provide Instruction, Learning and for the Common Good': An Analysis of the Reasons Given for Publishing Law Reports." Parts 1-2. *Law Librarian* 23, no. 2 (June 1992): 60-65; 23, no. 3 (Sept. 1992): 146-148.

188. Closen, Michael L., & Robert J. Dzielak. "The History and Influence of the Law Review Institution." *Akron Law Review* 30, no. 1 (Fall 1996): 15-54.

189. Cocks, Raymond. "Planning Law and Precedent: A Study in Twentieth-Century Law Reporting." In *Law Reporting in Britain* (Chantal Stebbings, ed.; London: Hambledon Press, 1995), 187-197.

190. Cohen, Daniel A. "The Story of Jason Fairbanks: Trial Reports and the Rise of Sentimental Fiction." *Legal Studies Forum* 17, no. 2 (1993): 119-132.

191. Cohen, Daniel A. "In Praise of Morris L. Cohen's *Bibliography of Early American Law*." *Law Library Journal* 104, no. 1 (Winter 2012): 25-32.

192. Cohen, Morris L., Edwin Wolf II, & William Jeffrey Jr. "Historical Development of the American Lawyer's Library." *Law Library Journal* 61, no. 4 (Nov. 1968): 440-462.

193. Cohen, Morris L., & Sharon Hamby [O'Connor]. "A Bibliography of the Early Reports of the Supreme Court of the United States." *Legal Reference Services Quarterly* 1, no. 2-3 (Summer/Fall 1981): 43-144.

194. Cohen, Morris L. "Blackstone at Yale." *Yale Law Report* 28 (1982): 18-20.

195. Cohen, Morris L. "Legal Literature in Colonial Massachusetts." In *Law in Colonial Massachusetts, 1630-1800: A Conference Held 6 and 7 November 1981* (Boston: Colonial Society of Massachusetts, 1984), 243-272.

196. Cohen, Morris L. "Legal Forms: From Clay to Computers." *Yale Law Report* 31 (1985): 25-28.

197. Cohen, Morris L. "Compiling an Historical Bibliography of American Law: Problems, Procedures and Prospects." *Legal Reference Services Quarterly* 9 (1989): 127-46.

198. Cohen, Morris L. "International Law Treatises in Early America." In *Essays in Honour of Jan Štěpán on the*

Occasion of His 80th Birthday (Zürich: Schulthess Polygraphischer Verlag, 1994), 321-326.

199. Cohen, Morris L., & Sharon Hamby O'Connor. *A Guide to the Early Reports of the Supreme Court of the United States.* Littleton, CO: F.B. Rothman, 1995.

200. Cohen, Morris L. *Bibliography of Early American Law.* 6 vols., and 2003 supplement. Buffalo, NY: William S. Hein & Co., 1998.

201. Cohen, Morris L. "Irish Influences on Early American Law Books: Authors, Printers and Subjects." *Irish Jurist* 36 (2001): 199-213.

202. Cohen, Morris L. *Juvenile Jurisprudence: Law in Children's Literature: An Exhibition Drawing in Part on the Betsy Beinecke Shirley Collection of American Children's Literature, January 30 through April 11, 2003.* New Haven, CT: Beinecke Rare Book and Manuscript Library, Yale University, 2003.

203. Cohen, Morris L. "English Legal Lexicographers after Rastell." In *Language and the Law: Proceedings of a Conference, December 6-8, 2001, Tarlton Law Library, The University of Texas at Austin* (Marlyn Robinson, ed.; Buffalo, N.Y.: William S. Hein & Co., 2003), 47-61.

204. Cohen, Morris L. "An Historical Overview of American Law Publishing." *International Journal of Legal Information* 31, no. 2 (Summer 2003): 168-178.

205. Cohen, Morris L. "Bibliography." In *Blackstone and His Commentaries: Biography, Law, History* (Wilfrid Prest, ed.; Oxford, UK: Hart Publishing, 2009), 217-228.

206. Columbia University. *Catalog of the Roman Law Collection of the Columbia Law School Library.* Boston: G.K. Hall, 1989.

207. Combe, David. "Civil Law." In *Collecting and Managing Rare Law Books: Papers Presented at a Conference Celebrating the Dedication of the New Tarlton Law Library, the University of Texas at Austin School of*

Law, January 7 & 8, 1981 (Roy M. Mersky & Stanley Ferguson, eds.; Dobbs Ferry, NY: Oceana Publications, 1981), 153-163.

208. Combe, David. "The Louisiana Lawyer's Roman-Law Library: Recollections of an Antiquarian Bibliophile." *Tulane Law Review* 70, no. 6 Part A (June 1996): 2003-2050.

209. Conley, J. A. "Doing It by the Book: Justice of the Peace Manuals and English Law in Eighteenth Century America." *Journal of Legal History* 6, no. 3 (Dec. 1985): 257-298.

210. Conte, Emanuele, & Magnus Ryan. "Codification in the Western Middle Ages." In *Diverging Paths? The Shapes of Power and Institutions in Medieval Christendom and Islam* (John Hudson & Ana Rodríguez, eds.; Leiden: Brill, 2014), 75-97.

211. Conte, Emanuele. "The Centre and the Margins of the Jungle of Glossed Manuscripts." *Rivista Internazionale di Diritto Comune* 32 (2021): 55-73.

212. Cook, Peter J. "Hywel Dda's Law-Books and the Welsh Legal Tradition." *Ius Commune* 18 (1991): 195-205.

213. Cooper, Byron D. "Anglo-American Legal Citation: Historical Development and Library Implications." *Law Library Journal* 75, no. 1 (Winter 1982): 3-33.

214. Cooper, Thomas. "Some Classics of Scottish Legal Literature: An Address Delivered to the Institute of Bankers in Scotland at Edinburgh on 29th October 1929." In Thomas Cooper, *Selected Papers, 1922-1954* (Edinburgh: Oliver & Boyd, 1957), 39-52.

215. Coquillette, Daniel R. "Legal Ideology and Incorporation I: The English Civilian Writers, 1523-1607." *Boston University Law Review* 61, no. 1 (Jan. 1981): 1-89.

216. Coquillette, Daniel R. "Legal Ideology and Incorporation II: Sir Thomas Ridley, Charles Molloy, and the Literary

Battle for the Law Merchant, 1607-1676." *Boston University Law Review* 61, no. 2 (Mar. 1981): 315-374.

217. Coquillette, Daniel R. "Legal Ideology and Incorporation III: Reason Regulated - The Post-Restoration English Civilians, 1653-1735." *Boston University Law Review* 67, no. 2 (Mar. 1987): 289-361.

218. Coquillette, Daniel R. *The Civilian Writers of Doctors' Commons, London: Three Centuries of Juristic Innovation in Comparative, Commercial and International Law.* Berlin: Duncker & Humblot, 1988.

219. Coquillette, Daniel R. "First Flower – The Earliest American Law Reports and the Extraordinary Josiah Quincy Jr. (1744-1775)." *Suffolk University Law Review* 30, no. 1 (1996): 1-34.

220. Corredera, Edward Jones, Mark Somos, *et al.* "Hugo Grotius's *De iure belli ac pacis*: A Report on the Worldwide Census of the First Edition (1625)." *Grotiana* 43, no. 1 (Aug. 2022): 208-235.

221. Corredera, Edward Jones, Mark Somos, *et al.* "Hugo Grotius's *De iure belli ac pacis*: A Report on the Worldwide Census of the Second Edition (1626)." *Grotiana* 43, no. 1 (Aug. 2022): 236-245.

222. Corredera, Edward Jones, Mark Somos, *et al.* "Hugo Grotius's *De iure belli ac pacis*: A Report on the Worldwide Census of the Third Edition (1631)." *Grotiana* 43, no. 1 (Aug. 2022): 246-272.

223. Corredera, Edward Jones, Mark Somos, *et al.* "*Hugo Grotius's De iure belli ac pacis*: A Report on the Worldwide Census of the Fourth Edition (1632, Janssonius)." *Grotiana* 43, no. 2 (Dec. 2022): 395-411.

224. Corredera, Edward Jones, Mark Somos, *et al.* "Hugo Grotius's *De iure belli ac pacis*: A Report on the Worldwide Census of the Fifth Edition (1632, Blaeu)." *Grotiana* 43, no. 2 (Dec. 2022): 412-436.

225. Corredera, Edward Jones, Mark Somos, *et al.* "Hugo Grotius's *De iure belli ac pacis*: A Report on the Worldwide Census of the Sixth Edition (1642, Blaeu)." *Grotiana* 43, no. 2 (Dec. 2022): 437-464.

226. Corredera, Edward Jones, Mark Somos, *et al.* "Hugo Grotius's *De iure belli ac pacis*: A Report on the Worldwide Census of the Seventh Edition (1646)." *Grotiana* 44, no. 1 (Aug. 2023): 154-180.

227. Corredera, Edward Jones, Mark Somos, *et al.* "Hugo Grotius's *De iure belli ac pacis*: Henricus Laurentius' Re-Issue (1647) of the 1631 Edition." *Grotiana* 44, no. 1 (Aug. 2023): 181-196.

228. Corredera, Edward Jones, Mark Somos, *et al.* "Hugo Grotius's *De iure belli ac pacis*: A Report on the Worldwide Census of the 1650 Edition." *Grotiana* 44, no. 1 (Aug. 2023): 197-216.

229. Cosgrove, Richard A. "Sir Thomas Erskine Holland and the Treatise Tradition: The Elements of Jurisprudence Revisited." In *Learning the Law: Teaching and the Transmission of Law in England, 1150-1900* (Jonathan Bush & Alain A. Wijffels, eds.; London: Hambledon Press, 1999), 397-406.

230. Coulson, Doug. "The Devil's Advocate and Legal Oratory in the *Processus Sathanae*." *Rhetorica* 38, no. 4 (Nov. 2016): 409-430.

231. Cowley, John D. "A Century of Law Booksellers in London, 1650-1750." *Law Times* 157, no. 4230 (26 Apr. 1924): 347-349.

232. Cowley, John D. "The Abridgements of the Statutes, 1481?-1551." *The Library: Transactions of the Bibliographical Society*, 4th series 12, no. 2 (Sept. 1931), 125-173.

233. Cowley, John D. *A Bibliography of Abridgments, Digests, Dictionaries and Indexes of English Law to the*

Year 1800. London: Quaritch, 1932. Reprinted: Holmes Beach, FL: Gaunt, 1979.

234. Craddock, Jerry R. *The Legislative Works of Alfonso X, el Sabio: A Critical Bibliography.* London: Grant & Cutler, 1986.

235. Crête, Raymonde, Sylvio Normand, & Thomas Copeland. "Law Reporting in Nineteenth Century Quebec." *Journal of Legal History* 16, no. 2 (Aug. 1995): 147-172.

236. Custer, Joseph A. "Case Western University Law School Library: 125 Years." *Law Library Journal* 112, no. 1 (Winter 2020): 47-93.

237. Custer, Lawrence B. "William Cumming: A Colonial Lawyer and His Library." *Journal of Southern Legal History* 3 (1994): 221-240.

238. Dabney, Laura C. "Citators: Past, Present and Future." *Legal Reference Services Quarterly* 27, nos. 2-3 (2008): 165-190.

239. Daniel, A. Mercer. "The Law Library of Howard University, 1867-1956." *Law Library Journal* 51, no. 3 (Aug. 1958): 202-215.

240. Danner, Richard A. "Legal Information and the Development of American Law: Writings on the Form and Structure of the Published Law." *Law Library Journal* 99, no. 2 (Spring 2007): 193-227.

241. Danner, Richard A. "Foreword: Oh, the Treatise!" *Michigan Law Review* 111, no. 6 (Apr. 2013): 821-834.

242. Danner, Richard A. "Influences of the Digest Classification System: What Can We Know?" *Legal Reference Services Quarterly* 33, no. 2 (2014): 117-156.

243. Danner, Richard A. "Law Libraries and Laboratories: The Legacies of Langdell and His Metaphor." *Law Library Journal* 107, no. 1 (Winter 2015): 7-55.

244. Danner, Richard A. "More than Decisions: Reviews of American Law Reports in the Pre-West Era." *Duke Law*

School Public Law & Legal Theory Series, no. 2015-27 (2015). https://ssrn.com/abstract=2622299

245. Danwerth, Otto. "The Circulation of Pragmatic Normative Literature in Spanish America (16th-17th Centuries)." In *Knowledge of the* Pragmatici*: Legal and Moral Theological Literature and the Formation of Early Modern Ibero-America* (Thomas Duve & Otto Danwerth, eds.; Leiden: Brill Nijhoff, 2020), 89-130.

246. Dart, Henry Plauché. "The Law Library of a Louisiana Lawyer in the Eighteenth Century." *Loyola Law Journal* (New Orleans) 6, no. 1 (Dec. 1924): 1-18.

247. Davies, Bernita J. "A History of the Law Library Journal." *Law Library Journal* 49, no. 2 (May 1956): 157-167.

248. Davies, Jon. "Aspects of Nineteenth-Century Legal Literature." *Cambrian Law Review* 29 (1998): 22-54.

249. Davies, Ross E. "The Original Law Journals." *The Green Bag*, 2nd ser., 12, no. 2 (Winter 2009): 187-217.

250. Davies, Ross E. "West's Words, Ho! Law Books by the Million, Plus a Few." *The Green Bag*, 2nd Ser., 14, no. 3 (Spring 2011): 303-310.

251. Davies, Ross E. "Marshall's Maps, the U.S. Reports, and the New Judicial Restraint." *The Green Bag*, 2nd ser., 15, no. 4 (Summer 2012): 443-462.

252. Davies, Ross E. "How West Law was Made: The Company, its Products, and its Promotions." *Charleston Law Review* 6, no. 2 (Winter 2012): 231-282.

253. Davies, Ross E. "Legal-Bibliographical Roots: Fragments of a *Green Bag* Origin Story." *The Green Bag*, 2nd ser., 24, no. 3 (Spring 2021), 253-272.

254. Davis, Donald R., Jr. "Law and 'Law Books' in the Hindu Tradition." *German Law Journal* 9, no. 3 (2008): 309-326.

255. Davis, Laurel. *Law Among Nations*. Boston: Boston College Law Library, 2012.

256. Davis, Laurel. *Francis Bacon: Of Law, Science, and Philosophy.* Boston: Boston College Law Library, 2013.

257. Davis, Laurel. *The Law in Postcards*. Boston: Boston College Law Library, 2014.

258. Davis, Laurel. *Exploring Magna Carta.* Boston: Boston College Law Library, 2015.

259. Davis, Laurel. *Discovering Cases: Year Books, Reporters & Beyond.* Boston: Boston College Law Library, 2017.

260. Davis, Laurel. *Don't Reinvent the Wheel: The History of Form Books in Anglo-American Legal Literature.* Boston: Boston College Law Library, 2017.

261. Davis, Laurel, & Katie Lewis. *The James S. Rogers Collection: Examining the Past to Inform the Future.* Boston: Boston College Law Library, 2018.

262. Davis, Laurel. *Dictionaries and the Law*. Boston: Boston College Law Library, 2019.

263. Davis, Laurel, & Mary Sarah Bilder. "The Library of Robert Morris, Antebellum Civil Rights Lawyer and Activist." *Law Library Journal* 111, no. 4 (Fall 2019): 461-508.

264. Davis, Laurel, & Mary Sarah Bilder. *Female Imprimatur: Women in the Lawbook Trade.* Boston: Boston College Law Library, 2020.

265. Davis, Laurel, & Melissa Grasso. *Summoning Shakespeare, Cicero, and Scripture: Epigraphs in Law Books.* Boston: Boston College Law Library, 2022.

266. Dawson, John P. "The Harvard Collections of Foreign Law: Changing Dimensions of Legal Study." *Harvard Library Bulletin* 16, no. 2 (Apr. 1968): 101-110.

267. Derrington, Roger. "The Modern Authorised Law Reports and Their Digests." *Queensland Legal Yearbook 2014*: 113-131. https://archive.sclqld.org.au/sclpub/

queensland-legal-yearbook/2014/queensland-legal-yearbook-2014.pdf

268. Devereux, E. J. *A Bibliography of John Rastell*. Montreal: McGill-Queen's University Press, 1999.

269. Devoti, Luciana. "A Medieval Puzzle: The 'Architecture' of the Page in Manuscripts and Incunabula of the Codex Justinianus." In *Trends in Statistical Codicology* (Marilena Maniaci, ed.; Boston: De Gruyter, 2022), 509-574.

270. Dewey, Scott Hamilton. "Growing Pains: The History of the UCLA Law Library, 1949-2000." *Law Library Journal* 108, no. 2 (Spring 2016): 217-236.

271. Diamond, Lucia. "Roman and Canon Law Research." *Legal Reference Services Quarterly* 20 (2001): 99-112.

272. Dietzman, Richard Priest. "The Kentucky Law Reports and Reporters." *Kentucky Law Journal* 16, no. 1 (Nov. 1927): 16-27.

273. Dingledy, Frederick W. "The *Corpus Juris Civilis*: A Guide to its History and Use." *Legal Reference Services Quarterly* 35, no. 4 (2016): 231-255.

274. Dingledy, Frederick W. "From Stele to Silicon: Publication of Statutes, Public Access to the Law, and the Uniform Electronic Legal Material Act." *Law Library Journal* 111, no. 2 (Spring 2019): 165-195.

275. Dippel, Horst. "Blackstone in Germany." In *Blackstone and His Commentaries: Biography, Law, History* (Wilfrid Prest, ed.; Oxford, UK: Hart Publishing, 2009), 199-214.

276. Dippel, Horst. "The Trap of Medium-Neutral Citation, or Why a Historical-Critical Edition of State Constitutions Is Necessary." *Law Library Journal* 103, no. 2 (Spring 2011): 219-231.

277. Dolezalek, Gero R. "Reports of the 'Rota' (14th-19th Centuries)." In *Judicial Records, Law Reports, and*

the Growth of Case Law (John H. Baker, ed.; Berlin: Duncker & Humblot, 1989), 69-100.

278. Dolezalek, Gero R. "Research on Manuscripts of the Corpus Iuris with Glosses Written during the 12th and Early 13th Centuries: State of Affairs." In *El dret comú y Catalunya: Actes del I.er Simposi Internacional, Barcelona, 25-26 de maig de 1990* (A. I. Ferreirós, ed.; Barcelona, 1991), 17-45.

279. Dolezalek, Gero R. "Research on Manuscripts of the Corpus Iuris with Glosses Written during the 12th and Early 13th Centuries: State of Affairs." In *Miscellanea Domenico Maffei dicata: Historia - ius - stadium*, vol. 1 (P. Weimar & A. Garcia y Garcia, eds.; Goldbach 1995), 143-171.

280. Dolezalek, Gero R. "Canon Law and Roman Law: Some Statistics on Manuscripts in the Vatican Library." In *A Ennio Cortese* (D. Maffei *et al.*, eds.; Roma 2001), 500-505.

281. Dolezalek, Gero R. *"Libri magistrorum* and the Transmission of Glosses in Legal Textbooks (12th and Early 13th Century)." In *Juristische Buchproduktion im Mittelalter* (Vincenzo Colli, ed.; Frankfurt: Vittorio Klostermann, 2002), 315-349.

282. Dolezalek, Gero R. "French Legal Literature Quoted by Scottish Lawyers 1550-1650." In *Mélanges en l'honneur d'Anne Lefebvre-Teillard* (Bernard d'Alteroche *et al.*, eds.; Paris: Éditions Panthéon-Assas, 2009), 375-391.

283. Dolezalek, Gero R. "Manuscript Dissemination of Juridical Literature after 1500: Malta, Scotland, and Other Small Jurisdictions." In *Honos alit artes: studi per il settantesimo compleanno di Mario Ascheri* (4 vols.; Paola Maffei & Gian Maria Varanini, eds.; Firenze: Firenze University Press, 2014), 3:42-49.

284. Dolezalek, Gero R. "Glosses and the Juridical Genre 'Apparatus glossarum' in the Middle Ages." *Rivista Internazionale di Diritto Comune* 32 (2021): 9-54.

285. Donahue, Charles, Jr. "Benvenuto Stracca's De Mercatura: Was There a Lex Mercatoria in Sixteenth-Century Italy?" In *From Lex Mercatoria to Commercial Law* (Vito Piergiovanni, ed.; Berlin: Duncker & Humblot, 2005), 69-116.

286. Dondorp, Harry, & Eltjo J. H. Schrage. "The Sources of Medieval Learned Law." In *The Creation of the Ius Commune: From Casus to Regula* (John W. Cairns & Paul J. du Plessis, eds.; Edinburgh, UK: Edinburgh University Press, 2010), 7-56.

287. Dowling, Shelley L. "The United States Supreme Court Library." In *Law Librarianship: Historical Perspectives* (Laura N. Gasaway & Michael G. Chiorazzi, eds.; Littleton, CO: F. B. Rothman, 1996), 3-41.

288. Doyle New York. *The New York City Bar Association Rare Book Collection*. New York: Doyle New York, 2014.

289. Doyle New York. *Rare Books, Autographs, Maps & Photographs: Including Property from the Rare Books Collection of the New York City Bar Association and an Important Frida Kahlo Archive*. New York: Doyle New York, 2015.

290. Drechsler, Stefan. "Marginalia in Medieval Western Scandinavian Law Manuscripts." *Das Mittelalter* 25, no. 1 (2020): 180-195.

291. Drechsler, Stefan. "Jón Halldórsson and Law Manuscripts of Western Iceland c. 1320-40." In *Dominican Resonances in Medieval Iceland: The Legacy of Bishop Jón Halldórsson of Skálholt* (Gunnar Harðarson & Karl G. Johansson, eds.; Leiden: Brill, 2021), 125-150, 317-329.

292. Drechsler, Stefan. "Production and Content of the Fourteenth-Century Norwegian Law Manuscript *Lundarbók*." In *Law | Book | Culture in the Middle Ages* (Thom Gobbitt, ed.; Leiden: Koninklijke Brill NV, 2021), 17-50.

293. Drechsler, Stefan. "Law Manuscripts from Fifteenth-Century Iceland." *Gripla* 32 (2021): 165-198. https://doi.org/10.33112/gripla.32.7

294. Drossbach, Gisela. "Prefaces in Canon Law Books." In *Inscribing Knowledge in the Medieval Book: The Power of Paratexts* (Rosalind Brown-Grant *et al.*, eds.; Berlin: De Gruyter, 2019), 21-45.

295. Dubber, Markus D. "Introduction: Putting the Legal Treatise in Its Place." In *Law Books in Action: Essays on the Anglo-American Legal Treatise* (Angela Fernandez & Markus D. Dubber, eds.; Oxford: Hart Publishing, 2012), 1-21.

296. Duffey, Denis P., Jr. "Genre and Authority: The Rise of Case Reporting in the Early United States." *Chicago-Kent Law Review* 74, no. 1 (1998): 263-275.

297. Duggan, Charles. *Twelfth-century Decretal Collections and Their Importance in English History.* London: Athlone Press, 1963.

298. Duggan, Charles. "Decretal Collections from Gratian's *Decretum* to the *Compilationes antiquae*: The Making of the New Case Law." In *The History of Medieval Canon Law in the Classical Period, 1140-1234: From Gratian to the Decretals of Gregory IX* (Wilfried Hartmann & Kenneth Pennington, eds.; Washington, DC: Catholic University of America Press, 2008), 246-292.

299. Dumbauld, Edward. *The Life and Legal Writings of Hugo Grotius.* Norman: University of Oklahoma Press, 1969.

300. Dunne, Gerald T. "Early Court Reporters." *Supreme Court Historical Society Yearbook* (1976): 61-72.

301. Dupont, Jerry. *The Common Law Abroad: Constitutional and Legal Legacy of the British Empire.* Littleton, CO: Fred B. Rothman Publications, 2001.

302. Dusil, Stephan. "The Decretum of Gratian: A Janus-Faced Collection." In *New Discourses in Medieval*

Canon Law Research: Challenging the Master Narrative (Christof Rolker, ed.; Leiden: Brill, 2019), 127-144.

303. Duve, Thomas. "Pragmatic Normative Literature and the Production of Normative Knowledge in the Early Modern Iberian Empires (16th-17th Centuries)." In *Knowledge of the* Pragmatici*: Legal and Moral Theological Literature and the Formation of Early Modern Ibero-America* (Thomas Duve & Otto Danwerth, eds.; Leiden: Brill Nijhoff, 2020), 1-39.

304. Dwan, Ralph H., & Ernest R. Feidler. "The Federal Statutes — Their History and Use." *Minnesota Law Review* 22, no. 7 (June 1938): 1008-1029.

305. Edwards, John Goronwy. *Hywel Dda and the Welsh Lawbooks*. Bangor: E. Thomas, Gwalia Printing Works, 1929.

306. Eller, Catherine Spicer. *The William Blackstone Collection in the Yale Law Library: A Bibliographical Catalogue*. New Haven: Yale University Press, 1938. Reprinted: New York: Lawbook Exchange, 1993.

307. Elliott, Lucile. "History of the Law Library." *North Carolina Law Review* 24, no. 3 (Apr. 1946): 402-413.

308. Elton, G. R. "The Sessional Printing of Statutes, 1484-1547." In *Wealth and Power in Tudor England: Essays Presented to S. T. Bindoff* (E. W. Ives *et al.*, eds.; London: Athlone Press, 1978), 68-86.

309. Emerson, John. "Did Blackstone Get the Gallic Shrug?" In *Blackstone and His Commentaries: Biography, Law, History* (Wilfrid Prest, ed.; Oxford, UK: Hart Publishing, 2009), 185-198.

310. Emery, Robert A. "The Albany Law School Journal: The Only Surviving Copy." *Law Library Journal* 89, no. 4 (Fall 1997): 463-466.

311. Emery, Robert A. "Selling to the Legal Market: Advertisements in the Early Harvard Law Review."

Legal Reference Services Quarterly 25, nos. 2-3 (2006): 141-146.

312. Emery, Robert A. "Dominick Blake's Criminal Law Treatise: A Sad Tale." *Legal Reference Services Quarterly* 30, no. 3 (2011): 231-236.

313. Eshleman, Michael O. "A History of the Digests." *Law Library Journal* 110, no. 2 (Spring 2018): 235-259.

314. Eska, Charlene M. "Varieties of Early Irish Legal Literature and the *Cáin Lánamna* Fragments." *Viator* 40, no. 1 (2009): 1-16.

315. Farmer, Lindsay. "Of Treatises and Textbooks: The Literature of the Criminal Law in Nineteenth-Century Britain." In *Law Books in Action: Essays on the Anglo-American Legal Treatise* (Angela Fernandez & Markus D. Dubber, eds.; Oxford: Hart Publishing, 2012), 145-164.

316. Fedynskyj, Jurij. "State Session Laws in Non-English Languages: A Chapter of American Legal History." *Indiana Law Journal* 46, no. 4 (Summer 1971): 463-479.

317. Feenstra, Robert, & C. J. D. Waal. *Seventeenth-Century Leyden Law Professors and Their Influence on the Development of the Civil Law: A Study of Bronchorst, Vinnius and Voet.* Amsterdam: North-Holland Pub. Co., 1975.

318. Feenstra, Robert, & Douglas J. Osler. *Bibliography of Jurists of the Northern Netherlands Active Outside the Dutch Universities to the Year 1811.* Amsterdam: Royal Netherlands Academy of Sciences, 2017.

319. Ferguson, F. S. "A Bibliography of the Works of Sir George Mackenzie, Lord Advocate, Founder of the Advocates' Library." *Edinburgh Bibliographical Society Transactions* 1 (1935-1938), 1-60.

320. Fernandez, Angela. "Albert Mayrand's Private Law Library: An Investigation of the Person, the Law of Persons, and Legal Personality in a Collection of Law

Books." *University of Toronto Law Journal* 53, no. 1 (Winter 2003): 37-64.

321. Fernandez, Angela. "Tapping Reeve, Coverture and America's First Legal Treatise." In *Law Books in Action: Essays on the Anglo-American Legal Treatise* (Angela Fernandez & Markus D. Dubber, eds.; Oxford: Hart Publishing, 2012), 63-81.

322. Fernandez, Angela. "Legal History as the History of Legal Texts." In *The Oxford Handbook of Legal History* (Markus D. Dubber & Christopher Tomlins, eds.; Oxford: Oxford University Press, 2018), 243-262.

323. Ferris, David A. *One Man's Books: The Library of Roscoe Pound.* Cambridge, MA: Harvard Law School Library, 1993.

324. Fidler, Ann. "'Till You Understand Them in Their Principal Features': Observations on Form and Function in Nineteenth-Century American Law Books." *Papers of the Bibliographical Society of America* 92 (Dec. 1998): 427-442.

325. Fiero, Maribel. "Codifying the Law: The Case of the Medieval Islamic West." In *Diverging Paths? The Shapes of Power and Institutions in Medieval Christendom and Islam* (John Hudson & Ana Rodríguez, eds.; Leiden: Brill, 2014), 98-118.

326. Figueira, Robert C. "Ricardus de Mores and his *Casus decretalium*: The Birth of a Canonistic Genre." In *Proceedings of the Eighth International Congress of Medieval Canon Law: San Diego, University of California at La Jolla, 21-27 August 1988* (Stanley Chodorow, ed.; Città del Vaticano: Biblioteca Apostolica Vaticana, 1992), 168-187.

327. Filiu, Vincenc, Dennis Kim-Prieto, & Teresa Miguel. "A Closer Look: A Symposium among Legal Historians and Law Librarians to Uncover the Spanish Roots of Louisiana Civil Law." *International Journal of Legal Information* 38, no. 3 (Winter 2010): 295-338.

328. Finkelman, Paul. *Slavery in the Courtroom: An Annotated Bibliography of American Cases*. Washington, DC: Library of Congress, 1985. Reprinted: Clark, NJ: The Lawbook Exchange, 1998.

329. Fiori, Antonia. "Roman Law Sources and Canonical Collections in the Early Middle Ages." *Bulletin of Medieval Canon Law* 34 (2017): 1-32.

330. Fischer, Carsten. "Through a Glass Darkly: English Common Law Seen through the Lens of the *Göttingische Gelehrte Anzeigen* (Eighteenth Century)." In *Common Law, Civil Law, and Colonial Law: Essays in Comparative Legal History from the Twelfth to the Twentieth Centuries* (William Eves, *et al.*, eds; Cambridge, UK: Cambridge University Press, 2021), 161-182.

331. Fishman, Joel. "Catalogue of Modern Law Books, 1855." *Legal Reference Services Quarterly* 13, no. 2 (1994): 127-142.

332. Fishman, Joel. "The History of Statutory Compilations in Pennsylvania." *Law Library Journal* 86, no. 3 (Summer 1994): 559-596.

333. Fishman, Joel. "The Reports of the Supreme Court of Pennsylvania." *Law Library Journal* 87, no. 4 (Fall 1995): 643-693.

334. Fishman, Joel. "History of the Court Reporter in the Appellate Courts of Pennsylvania." *Widener Journal of Public Law* 7, no. 1 (1997): 1-38.

335. Fishman, Joel. "The Digests of Pennsylvania." *Law Library Journal* 90, no. 3 (1998): 481-508.

336. Fishman, Joel. "An Early Pennsylvania Legal Periodical: The *Pennsylvania Law Journal*, 1842-1848." *American Journal of Legal History* 45, no. 1 (Jan. 2001): 22-50.

337. Fishman, Joel. "Celebrating a Diamond Anniversary: Pennsylvania Bar Association Quarterly Volumes 1-74 (1929-2003): A History." *Pennsylvania Bar Association Quarterly* 75 (Apr. 2004): 66-78.

338. Fishman, Joel. "Citators of Pennsylvania." *Unbound: An Annual Review of Legal History and Rare Books* 1 (2008): 1-19. https://www.aallnet.org/lhrbsis/resources-publications/unbound/

339. Fishman, Joel. "The Court Reporters of the Supreme Court of Pennsylvania." *Unbound: A Review of Legal History and Rare Books* 2 (2009): 1-20. https://www.aallnet.org/lhrbsis/resources-publications/unbound/

340. Fishman, Joel. "A Failed Mid-Nineteenth Century Pennsylvania Legal Periodical/Newspaper: *Olwine's Law Journal* December 29, 1849 to May 18, 1850." *Unbound: A Review of Legal History and Rare Books* 2 (2009): 37-44. https://www.aallnet.org/lhrbsis/resources-publications/unbound/

341. Fishman, Joel. "The George T. Bisel Company and Its Publications (1875-2011)." *Unbound: An Annual Review of Legal History and Rare Books* 5 (2012): 29-60. https://www.aallnet.org/lhrbsis/resources-publications/unbound/

342. Fishman, Joel. "Law Book Catalog of Patrick Byrne, Philadelphia Bookseller, 1802." *Unbound: A Review of Legal History and Rare Books* 9 (2016): 69-110. https://www.aallnet.org/lhrbsis/resources-publications/unbound/

343. Fishman, Joel. "Third Circuit Court Reports (1789-1879)." *Law Library Journal* 108, no. 4 (Fall 2016): 623-654.

344. Fitzpatrick, John T. "The Session Laws of the State of New York." *Law Library Journal* 13, no. 4 (Jan. 1921): 80-86.

345. Fitzpatrick, John T. "Chancellor Kent's Law Library." *Law Library Journal* 21, no. 1 (Apr. 1928): 9-11.

346. Ford, J. D. "William Welwod's Treatises on Maritime Law." *Journal of Legal History* 34, no. 2 (Aug. 2013): 172-210.

347. *The Formation and Transmission of Western Legal Culture: 150 Books That Made the Law in the Age of Printing.* Serge Dauchy *et al.*, eds. Cham, Switzerland: Springer, 2016.

348. Fowler-Magerl, Linda. *Ordines iudiciarii and Libelli de ordine iudiciorum (From the Middle of the Twelfth to the End of the Fifteenth Century).* Turnhout, Belgium: Brepols, 1994.

349. Franklin, Mitchell. "Libraries of Edward Livingston and of Moreau Lislet." *Tulane Law Review* 15, no. 3 (1941): 401-414.

350. Franklin, Mitchell. "Library of Michel de Armas." *Louisiana Law Review* 4, no. 4 (1941-1942): 573-585.

351. Franklin, Mitchell. "The Library of Christian Roselius and Alfred Phillips." *Louisiana Law Review* 23, no. 4 (June 1963): 704-721.

352. Free Library of Philadelphia. *Catalog of the Hampton L. Carson Collection Illustrative of the Growth of the Common Law, in the Free Library of Philadelphia.* 2 vols. Boston: G.K. Hall, 1962.

353. Frey, Emil F., & David A. Kronick. "Landmark Books in Legal Medicine: A Checklist of Forensic and Medico-Legal Books to 1900." In *Collecting and Managing Rare Law Books: Papers Presented at a Conference Celebrating the Dedication of the New Tarlton Law Library, the University of Texas at Austin School of Law, January 7 & 8, 1981* (Roy M. Mersky & Stanley Ferguson, eds.; Dobbs Ferry, NY: Oceana Publications, 1981), 381-410.

354. Friend, William Lawrence, Jr. "A Survey of Anglo-American Legal Bibliography." *Law Library Journal* 33, no. 1 (Jan. 1940): 1-17.

355. Friend, William Lawrence, Jr. *Anglo-American Legal Bibliographies: An Annotated Guide.* Washington: U.S. G.P.O., 1944.

356. Frońska, Joanna. "Memory and the Making of Images: A Case of a Legal Manuscript." *Manuscripta* 54, no. 1 (2010): 1-20.

357. Frońska, Joanna. "Turning the Pages of Legal Manuscripts: Reading and Remembering the Law." In *Meaning in Motion: Semantics of Movement in Medieval Art* (Nino Zchomelidse & Giovanni Freni, eds.; Princeton, NJ: Princeton University Press, 2011), 191-214.

358. Frońska, Joanna. "The Memory of Roman Law in an Illuminated Manuscript of Justinian's Digest." In *Memory and Commemoration in Medieval Culture* (Elma Brenner, Meredith Cohen & Mary Franklin-Brown, eds.; Farnham, UK: Ashgate, 2013), 163-179.

359. Frońska, Joanna. "Writing in the Margin – Drawing in the Margin: Reading Practices of Medieval Jurists." In *Inscribing Knowledge in the Medieval Book: The Power of Paratexts* (Rosalind Brown-Grant *et al.*, eds.; Berlin: De Gruyter, 2019), 141-159.

360. Fruchtman, Gail H. "The History of the Los Angeles County Law Library." *Law Library Journal* 84, no. 4 (Fall 1992): 687-705. Reprinted: *Law Librarianship: Historical Perspectives* (Laura N. Gasaway & Michael G. Chiorazzi, eds.; Littleton, CO: F. B. Rothman, 1996), 163-181.

361. Gaebler, Hans D. "The Printing of Wisconsin Session Laws, 1836-1838." *Law Library Journal* 33, no. 2 (Mar. 1940): 56-59.

362. Gaines, Philip. "Writing the Discursive Proto-Culture of Modern Anglo-American Trial Advocacy: Edward William Cox's *The Advocate*." *American Journal of Legal History* 51, no. 2 (Apr. 2011): 333-358.

363. Galbraith, V. H. "The Modus Tenendi Parliamentum." *Journal of the Warburg and Courtauld Institutes* 16, nos. 1/2 (1953): 81-99.

364. García Martín, Javier. "Legal Authorities in Castilian Courts' Practice: *Decisiones* and *Consilia* to Study the *Arbitrium Iudicis*." In *Authorities in Early Modern Law Courts* (Guido Rossi, ed.; Edinburgh: Edinburgh University Press, 2021), 50-83.

365. Garnett, George. "'The Ould Fields': Law and History in the Prefaces to Sir Edward Coke's *Reports*." *Journal of Legal History* 34, no. 3 (Dec. 2013): 245-284.

366. Gerken, Joseph L. *The Invention of Legal Research.* Getzville, NY: William S. Hein & Co., 2016.

367. Gibbs, Robert. "The Development of the Illustration of Legal Manuscripts by Bolognese Illuminators between 1241 and 1298." In *Juristische Buchproduktion im Mittelalter* (Vincenzo Colli, ed.; Frankfurt am Main: Vittorio Klostermann, 2002), 173-218.

368. Gibbs, Robert. "Trees of Consanguinity and Affinity (ca. 1310-30)." In *Medieval Italy: Texts in Translation* (Katherine L. Jansen et *al.*, eds; Philadelphia: University of Pennsylvania Press, 2009), 438-440.

369. Gibbs, Robert. "The 13th- and 14th-Century Illuminated Statutes of Bologna in their Socio-political Context." In *Von der Ordnung zur Norm: Statuten in Mittelalter und Früher Neuzeit* (Gisela Drossbach, ed.; Paderborn: Schöningh, 2010), 183-200.

370. Girard, Philip. "Themes and Variations in Early Canadian Legal Culture: Beamish Murdoch and his *Epitome of the Laws of Nova-Scotia*." *Law and History Review* 11, no. 1 (Spring 1993): 101-144.

371. Girard, Philip. "'Of Institutes and Treatises': Blackstone's Commentaries, Kent's Commentaries and Murdoch's Epitome of the Laws of Nova-Scotia." In *Law Books in Action: Essays on the Anglo-American Legal Treatise* (Angela Fernandez & Markus D. Dubber, eds.; Oxford: Hart Publishing, 2012), 43-62.

372. Girvin, Stephen D. "Law Reporting: Menzies Reports, Precedent and Legal Sources at the Cape Colony in the Nineteenth Century." *Tijdschrift voor Rechtsgeschiedenis / Legal History Review* 63, nos. 1-2 (Jan. 1995): 103-118.

373. Giuliani, Adolfo. "Civilian Treatises on Presumptions, 1580-1620." In *The Law of Presumptions: Essays in Comparative Legal History* (R. H. Helmholz & W. David H. Sellar, eds.; Berlin: Duncker & Humblot, 2009), 22-71.

374. Glasier, Gilson G. "Early American Periodicals." *American Bar Association Journal* 28, no. 9 (Sept. 1942): 615-617.

375. Gobbitt, Thom. "Liutprand's Prologues in the *Edictus Langobardorum.*" In *Law | Book | Culture in the Middle Ages* (Thom Gobbitt, ed.; Leiden: Koninklijke Brill NV, 2021), 71-97.

376. Goodrich, Peter. "Satirical Legal Studies: From the Legists to the *Lizard.*" *Michigan Law Review* 103, no. 3 (Dec. 2004): 397-517.

377. Goodrich, Peter. *Legal Emblems and the Art of Law: Obiter Depicta as the Vision of Governance*. New York, NY: Cambridge University Press, 2014.

378. Goodrich, Peter. "The Emblem Book and Common Law." In *The Oxford Handbook of English Law and Literature, 1500-1700* (Lorna Hutson, ed.; Oxford; New York: Oxford University Press, 2017), 142-162.

379. Gordan, John D., III. "John Nutt: Trade Publisher and Printer 'In the Savoy.'" *The Library: Transactions of the Bibliographical Society*, 7th series 15, no. 3 (Sept. 2014): 243-260.

380. Gordan, John D., III. "Publishing Robinson's *Reports of Cases Argued and Determined in the High Court of Admiralty.*" *Law and History Review* 32, no. 3 (Aug. 2014): 525-573.

124

381. Gordan, John D., III. "Pirates on the Hudson: Copyright Broadsides in the pre-Civil War Law Book Trade." *Unbound: A Review of Legal History and Rare Books* 12, no. 2 (Winter/Spring 2021): 19-70. https://www.aallnet.org/lhrbsis/resources-publications/unbound/

382. Gordon, Edward. "Grotius and the Freedom of the Seas in the Seventeenth Century." *Willamette Journal of International Law & Dispute Resolution* 16, no. 2 (Winter 2008): 252-269.

383. Gordon, William M. "Stair's Use of Roman Law." In *Law-Making and Law-Makers in British History: Papers Presented to the Edinburgh Legal History Conference, 1977* (Alan Harding, ed.; London: Royal Historical Society, 1980), 120-126.

384. Gordon, William M. "Stair, Grotius and the Sources of Stair's Institutions." In *Satura Roberto Feenstra: sexagesimum quintum annum aetatis complenti ab alumnis collegis amicis oblata* (J. A. Ankum *et al.*, eds.; Fribourg, Switzerland: Éditions Universitaires, 1985), 571-583.

385. Grabar, V. E. *The History of International Law in Russia, 1647-1917: A Bio-bibliographical Study.* William E. Butler, translator. Oxford: Clarendon Press, 1990.

386. Graham, Howard Jay. "The Rastells and the Printed English Law Book of the Renaissance." *Law Library Journal* 47, no. 1 (Feb. 1954): 6-25.

387. Graham, Howard Jay. "John G. Marvin and the Founding of American Legal Bibliography." *Law Library Journal* 48, no. 3 (1955): 194-211.

388. Graham, Howard Jay, & J. W. Heckel. "The Book That 'Made' the Common Law: The First Printing of Fitzherbert's *La Graunde Abridgement*, 1514-1516." *Law Library Journal* 51, no. 2 (May 1958): 100-116.

389. Graham, Howard Jay. "A Legal Bibliographer in the Gold Rush." *Law Library Journal* 56, no. 3 (Aug. 1963): 247-254.

390. Graham, Howard Jay. "'Our Tong Maternall Maruellously Amendyd and Augmentyd': The First Englishing and Printing of the Medieval Statutes at Large, 1530-1533." *UCLA Law Review* 13, no. 1 (Nov. 1965): 58-98.

391. Greenlee, Edwin J. "The University of Pennsylvania Law Review: 150 Years of History," *University of Pennsylvania Law Review* 150, no. 6 (June 2002): 1875-1904.

392. Greer, Desmond. "Crime, Justice and Legal Literature in Nineteenth-Century Ireland." *Irish Jurist* 37 (2002): 241-268.

393. Gregory, Helen. *Capturing Law and History: One Hundred Years of Queensland Law Reporting*. Brisbane: Supreme Court of Queensland Library, 2007.

394. Groot, Gerard-René de, & Agustín Parise. "Anthoine de Saint-Joseph: A Nineteenth-Century Paladin for the Development of Comparative Legislation." In *Ten definitieven recht doende ... Louis Berkvens amicorum* (Bram Van Hofstraeten *et al.*, eds.; Maastricht: Koninklijk Limburgs Geschied- en Oudheidkundig Genootschap 2018), 70-92.

395. Grossman, George S. *Legal Research: Historical Foundations of the Electronic Age*. New York: Oxford University Press, 1994.

396. Grossman, George S. "Early American Legal Lexicographers." In *Language and the Law: Proceedings of a Conference, December 6-8, 2001, Tarlton Law Library, The University of Texas at Austin* (Marlyn Robinson, ed.; Buffalo, N.Y.: William S. Hein & Co., 2003), 63-91.

397. Gruben, Karl T., & James E. Hambleton. *A Reference Guide to Texas Law and Legal History: Sources and*

Documentation. 2nd ed. Austin, TX: Butterworth Legal Publishers, 1987. Revised edition of Marion O. Boner, *A Reference Guide to Texas Law and Legal History: Sources and Documentation* (Austin, TX: University of Texas Press, 1976).

398. Gummere, John S. "Some Noted Trials in Connecticut: A Bibliography." *Law Library Journal* 30, no. 5 (Nov. 1937): 529-539.

399. Günzl, Clara. "Case Law in Germany: The Significance of Seuffert's *Archiv*." In *Common Law, Civil Law, and Colonial Law: Essays in Comparative Legal History from the Twelfth to the Twentieth Centuries* (William Eves, *et al.*, eds; Cambridge, UK: Cambridge University Press, 2021), 206-235.

400. Hanson, F. Allan. "From Key Numbers to Keywords: How Automation Has Transformed the Law." *Law Library Journal* 94, no. 4 (Fall 2002): 563-600.

401. Harding, Alan. "Legislators, Lawyers and Lawbooks." In *Lawyers and Laymen: Studies in the History of Law Presented to Professor Dafydd Jenkins on His Seventy-Fifth Birthday, Gwyl Ddewi 1986* (T. M. Charles-Edwards *et al.*, eds.; Cardiff: University of Wales Press, 1986), 237-257.

402. Hargrett, Lester. *A Bibliography of the Constitutions and Laws of the American Indians*. Cambridge, MA: Harvard University Press, 1947. Reprinted: Clark, NJ: Lawbook Exchange, 2003.

403. Harrington, William G. "A Brief History of Computer-Assisted Legal Research." *Law Library Journal* 77, no. 3 (1984-85): 543-556.

404. Harris, Michael. "Trials and Criminal Biographies: A Case Study in Distribution." In *Sale and Distribution of Books from 1700* (Robin Meyers & Michael Harris, eds.; Oxford: Oxford Polytechnic Press, 1982), 1-36.

405. Harris, Michael H. "The Frontier Lawyer's Library: Southern Indiana, 1800-1850, as a Test Case." *American Journal of Legal History* 16, no. 3 (July 1972): 239-251.

406. Harvey, David. *The Law Emprynted and Englysshed: The Printing Press as an Agent of Change in Law and Legal Culture 1475-1642*. London: Bloomsbury Publishing, 2015.

407. Hassall, W. O., ed. *A Catalogue of the Library of Sir Edward Coke*. New Haven: Yale University Press, 1950.

408. Hayaert, Valérie. "Emblems." In *The Oxford Handbook of Law and Humanities* (Simon Stern *et al.*, eds.; New York: Oxford University Press, 2020), 757-778.

409. Hayes, Kevin J. "The Law Library of a Working Attorney: The Example of Patrick Henry." In *"Esteemed bookes of lawe" and the Legal Culture of Early Virginia* (Warren M. Billings & Brent Tarter, eds.; Charlottesville: University of Virginia Press, 2017), 137-156.

410. Hays, Gregory. "The Library of Hélion Jouffroy: A Survey and Some Additional Identifications." *Quaerendo* 47, nos. 3-4 (Dec. 2017): 199-221.

411. Heller, James S. "America's First Law School Library: A History of the College of William and Mary's Marshall-Wythe Law Library, 1779-1995." In *Law Librarianship: Historical Perspectives* (Laura N. Gasaway & Michael G. Chiorazzi, eds.; Littleton, CO: F. B. Rothman, 1996), 43-76.

412. Helmholz, Richard H. "Records and Reports: The English Ecclesiastical Courts." In *Case Law in the Making: The Techniques and Methods of Judicial Records and Law Reports* (Alain A. Wijffels, ed.; Berlin: Duncker & Humblot, 1997), 1:83-98.

413. Helmholz, Richard H. "The Canon Law." In *The Cambridge History of the Book in Britain, Volume III, 1400-1557*, (Lotte Hellinga & J. B. Trapp, eds.;

Cambridge: Cambridge University Press, 1999), 791-806.

414. Heltzel, Virgil B. "Ferdinando Pulton, Elizabethan Legal Editor." *Huntington Library Quarterly* 11, no. 1 (Nov. 1947): 77-79.

415. Henderson, Edith G. "Legal Literature and the Impact of Printing on the English Legal Profession." *Law Library Journal* 68, no. 3 (Aug. 1975): 288-293.

416. Hening, R. Neil. "A Handbook for All: William Waller Hening's *The New Virginia Justice*." In *"Esteemed bookes of lawe" and the Legal Culture of Early Virginia* (Warren M. Billings & Brent Tarter, eds.; Charlottesville: University of Virginia Press, 2017), 179-193.

417. Hepburn, Jasmin. "A Lawyer and His Sources: Nicolas Bohier and Legal Practice in Sixteenth-Century France." In *Reassessing Legal Humanism and Its Claims: Petere Fontes?* (Paul J. du Plessis & John W. Cairns, eds.; Edinburgh: Edinburgh University Press, 2016), 244-281.

418. Hershenzon, Daniel. "The Economy of Legal Images and Legal Texts in Sixteenth-Century Law Books: The Case of Praxis Crimins Presequendi." *Comitatus: A Journal of Medieval and Renaissance Studies* 36 (2005): 68-92.

419. Hespanha, Antonio Manuel. "Form and Content in Early Modern Legal Books: Bridging the Gap Between Material Bibliography and the History of Legal Thought." *Rechtsgeschichte (Rg)* 12 (2008): 12-50.

420. Hessler, John. "Editing Justinian's Corpus: A Study of the Paul Krueger Archive." *Law Library Journal* 103, no. 3 (Summer 2011): 459-472.

421. Heutger, Viola, Bastiaan van der Velden, & Laurens Winkel. "*De iure belli ac pacis*, the Copy of Christoph Besold (1577-1638)." *Grotiana* 35, no. 1 (Dec. 2014): 191-195.

422. Hicks, Frederick C. *Men and Books Famous in the Law*. Rochester, NY: Lawyers Co-operative, 1921. Reprinted: New York: Lawbook Exchange, 1992.

423. Hicks, Frederick C. "The Modern Medusa." *Law Library Journal* 14, no. 1 (Apr. 1921): 7-14.

424. Hicks, Frederick C. "Odor of Sanctity." *Law Library Journal* 30, no. 3 (July 1937): 415-425.

425. Hilyerd, William A. "Hi Superman, I'm a Lawyer: A Guide to Attorneys (and Other Legal Professionals) Portrayed in American Comic Books: 1910-2007." *Widener Law Review* 15 (2009-2010): 159-196.

426. Hobson, Charles F. "St. George Tucker: Judge, Legal Scholar, and Reformer of Virginia Law." In *"Esteemed bookes of lawe" and the Legal Culture of Early Virginia* (Warren M. Billings & Brent Tarter, eds.; Charlottesville: University of Virginia Press, 2017), 195-220.

427. Hoeflich, Michael H. "A Seventeenth Century Roman Law Bibliography: Jacques Godefroy and His *Bibliotheca Juris Civilis Romani*." *Law Library Journal* 75, no. 4 (Fall 1982): 514-528.

428. Hoeflich, Michael H. "Law Beyond Byzantium: The Evidence of Palimpsests." *Zeitschrift der Savigny-Stiftung für Rechtsgeschichte: Germanistische Abteilung* 104, no. 1 (1987), 261-267.

429. Hoeflich, Michael H. "Law in the Republican Classroom." *University of Kansas Law Review* 43, no. 4 (July 1995): 711-734.

430. Hoeflich, Michael H. "Vinnius and the Anglo-American Legal World: A Study in the Distribution and Use of a Dutch Civilian Author in the Common Law World." *Zeitschrift der Savigny-Stiftung für Rechtsgeschichte: Romanistische Abteilung* 114 (1997): 345-368.

431. Hoeflich, Michael H. "Bibliographical Perspectives on Roman and Civil Law." *Law Library Journal* 89, no. 1 (Winter 1997): 41-54.

432. Hoeflich, Michael H. "Legal History and the History of the Book: Variations on a Theme." *University of Kansas Law Review* 46, no. 3 (Apr. 1998): 415-431.

433. Hoeflich, Michael H. "John Livingston and the Business of Law in Nineteenth-Century America." *American Journal of Legal History* 44, no. 4 (Oct. 2000): 347-368.

434. Hoeflich, Michael H., & Louis de la Vergne. "Gustavus Schmidt: His Life & His Library." *Roman Legal Tradition* 1 (2002): 112-122.

435. Hoeflich, Michael H. "The Lawyer as Pragmatic Reader: The History of Legal Common-Placing." *Arkansas Law Review* 55, no. 1 (2002): 87-122.

436. Hoeflich, Michael H., & Lawrence Jenab. "The Origins of the Kansas Law Review." *University of Kansas Law Review* 50, no. 2 (Jan. 2002): 375-382.

437. Hoeflich, Michael H. "Translation and the Reception of Foreign Law in the Antebellum United States." *American Journal of Comparative Law* 50, no. 4 (Fall 2002): 753-775.

438. Hoeflich, Michael H. "Lawyers, Books and Papers." *The Green Bag*, 2nd ser., 5, no. 2 (Winter 2002): 163-172.

439. Hoeflich, Michael H. "Auctions and the Distribution of Law Books in Antebellum America." *Proceedings of the American Antiquarian Society* 113, no. 1 (Apr. 2003): 135-161.

440. Hoeflich, Michael H., & Karen S. Beck. *Catalogues of Early American Law Libraries: The 1846 Auction Catalogue of Joseph Story's Library.* Austin, TX: Jamail Center for Legal Research, University of Texas at Austin, 2004.

441. Hoeflich, Michael H. "Annals of Legal Bibliography: J. G. Marvin." *Law Library Journal* 96, no. 2 (Spring 2004): 333-344.

442. Hoeflich, Michael H., Louis V. de la Vergne, & Kjell Å Modéer. *The 1877 Sale Catalogue of Gustavus Schmidt's*

Library. Austin, TX: Jamail Center for Legal Research, the University of Texas at Austin, 2005.

443. Hoeflich, Michael H. *Subscription Publishing and the Sale of Law Books in Antebellum America*. Austin, TX: Jamail Center for Legal Research, the University of Texas at Austin, 2007.

444. Hoeflich, Michael H., & Jasonne M. Grabher. "The Establishment of Normative Legal Texts: The Beginnings of the *Ius Commune*." In *The History of Medieval Canon Law in the Classical Period, 1140-1234: From Gratian to the Decretals of Gregory IX* (Wilfried Hartmann & Kenneth Pennington, eds.; Washington, DC: Catholic University of America Press, 2008), 1-21.

445. Hoeflich, Michael H. "Law Blanks & Form Books: A Chapter in the Early History of Document Production." *The Green Bag*, 2nd ser., 11, no. 2 (Winter 2008): 189-201.

446. Hoeflich, Michael H. "American Blackstones." In *Blackstone and His Commentaries: Biography, Law, History* (Wilfrid Prest, ed.; Oxford, UK: Hart Publishing, 2009), 171-184.

447. Hoeflich, Michael H. *Legal Publishing in Antebellum America*. New York: Cambridge University Press, 2010.

448. Hoeflich, Michael H., & William E. Butler. *The Syllabi: Genesis of the National Reporter System*. Clark, NJ: Lawbook Exchange, 2011.

449. Hoeflich, Michael H. *The Law in Postcards & Ephemera 1890-1962*. Clark, NJ: Lawbook Exchange, 2012.

450. Hoeflich, Michael H. "Law Book Hunting in the Heartland: A Life in Books." *University of Kansas Law Review* 68, no. 4 (May 2020): 727-742.

451. Hoeflich, Michael H., & Sydney Buckley. "International Law Texts in American Law Libraries: 1785-1900." *Jus Gentium: Journal of International Legal History* 6, no. 1 (Jan. 2021): 171-190.

452. Hoeflich, Michael H. "The Remarkable Civil Law Library of Judge John Purviance." *Jus Gentium: Journal of International Legal History* 7, no. 1 (Jan. 2022): 25-70.

453. Hoeflich, Michael H. "'Pedigrees in the Ownership of Law Books': Lawyers' Networks, Celebrity, and the Importance of Provenance in Nineteenth-Century Law." *American Journal of Legal History* 62, no. 1 (Mar. 2022): 41-65.

454. Hogan, John C. "Joseph Story's *Encyclopedia Americana* 'Law Articles.'" *Law Library Journal* 48, no. 2 (May 1955): 117-135.

455. Holdsworth, William S. "Charles Viner and the Abridgments of English Law." *Law Quarterly Review* 39, no. 1 (Jan. 1923): 17-45. Reprinted: *Mississippi Law Review* 1, no. 3 (Feb. 1923).

456. Holdsworth, William S., & James Richard Atkin. *Sources and Literature of English Law*. Oxford: Clarendon Press, 1925.

457. Holdsworth, William S. *Some Makers of English Law: The Tagore Lectures 1937-38.* Cambridge, UK: University Press, 1938.

458. Holdsworth, William S. "Law Reporting in the Nineteenth and Twentieth Centuries." In *Essays in Law and History* (A. L. Goodhart & H. G. Hanbury, eds.; Oxford: Clarendon Press, 1946), 284-292.

459. Holdsworth, William S. "Literature in Law Books." In *Essays in Law and History* (A. L. Goodhart & H. G. Hanbury, eds.; Oxford: Clarendon Press, 1946), 219-237.

460. Hollond, H. A. "English Legal Authors before 1700." *Cambridge Law Journal* 9, no. 3 (1947): 292-329.

461. Holt, James Clarke. *Magna Carta and Medieval Government*. London: Hambledon Press, 1985.

462. Honoré, Tony. "The Background to Justinian's Codification." *Tulane Law Review* 48, no. 4 (June 1974): 859-893.

463. Honoré, Tony. "How Tribonian Organised the Compilation of Justinian's Digest." *Zeitschrift der Savigny-Stiftung für Rechtsgeschichte: Romanistische Abteilung* 121, no. 1 (2004): 1-43.

464. Honoré, Tony. *Justinian's Digest: Character and Compilation.* Oxford, UK: Oxford University Press, 2010.

465. Honores, Renzo. "Presence and Use of Pragmatic Legal Literature in Habsburg Peru (16th-17th Centuries)." In *Knowledge of the* Pragmatici*: Legal and Moral Theological Literature and the Formation of Early Modern Ibero-America* (Thomas Duve & Otto Danwerth, eds.; Leiden: Brill Nijhoff, 2020), 131-150.

466. Horwitz, Morton J. "Treatise Literature." *Law Library Journal* 69, no. 4 (Nov. 1976): 460-461.

467. Hoyos, Roman J. "A Province of Jurisprudence? Invention of a Law of Constitutional Conventions." In *Law Books in Action: Essays on the Anglo-American Legal Treatise* (Angela Fernandez & Markus D. Dubber, eds.; Oxford: Hart Publishing, 2012), 108-126.

468. Hudon, Edward G. "The Library Facilities of the Supreme Court of the Unites States: A Historical Study." Parts I-II. *University of Detroit Law Journal* 34, no. 2 (Nov. 1956): 181-206; 34, no. 3 (1957): 317-332.

469. Hulsebosch, Daniel J. "An Empire of Law: Chancellor Kent and the Revolution in Books in the Early Republic." *Alabama Law Review* 60, no. 2 (2009): 377-424.

470. Huws, Daniel. *The Medieval Codex with Reference to the Welsh Law Books.* Aberystwyth: Canolfan Uwchefrydiau Cymreig a Cheltaidd, Coleg Prifysgol Cymru, 1982.

134

471. Ibbetson, David J. "Law Reporting in the 1590s." In *Law Reporting in Britain* (Chantal Stebbings, ed.; London: Hambledon Press, 1995), 73-88.

472. Ibbetson, David J. "Coventry's Reports." *Journal of Legal History* 16, no. 3 (Dec. 1995): 281-303.

473. Ibbetson, David J., & Serge Dauchy. "Case-Law and Judicial Precedents in Mediaeval and Early-Modern England." In *Auctoritates, xenia R.C. van Caenegem oblata: Law Making and Its Authors* (Serge Dauchy et al., eds.; Brussels: Wetenschappelijk Comité voor Rechtsgeschiedenis, Koninklijke Academie voor Wetenschappen, Letteren en Schone Kunsten van België, 1997), 55-68.

474. Ibbetson, David J., & Alain A. Wijffels. "Case Law in the Making: The Techniques and Methods of Judicial Records and Law Reports." In *Case Law in the Making: The Techniques and Methods of Judicial Records and Law Reports* (Alain A. Wijffels, ed.; Berlin: Duncker & Humblot, 1997), 1:13-35.

475. Ibbetson, David J. "Reports and Records in Early-Modern Common Law." In *Case Law in the Making: The Techniques and Methods of Judicial Records and Law Reports* (Alain A. Wijffels, ed.; Berlin: Duncker & Humblot, 1997), 1:55-68.

476. Ibbetson, David J. "Legal Printing and Legal Doctrine." *Irish Jurist* 35 (2000): 345-354.

477. Ibbetson, David J. "Sources of Law from the Republic to the Dominate." In *The Cambridge Companion to Roman Law* (David Johnston, ed.; Cambridge: Cambridge University Press, 2015), 25-44.

478. Ibbetson, David J. "Humanism and Law in Elizabethan England: The Annotations of Gabriel Harvey." In *Reassessing Legal Humanism and Its Claims: Petere Fontes?* (Paul J. du Plessis & John W. Cairns, eds.; Edinburgh: Edinburgh University Press, 2016), 282-295.

479. Ibbetson, David J. "Errores in Camera Scaccarii." In *English Legal History and Its Sources: Essays in Honour of Sir John Baker*, (David Ibbetson *et al.*; eds.; Cambridge, UK: Cambridge University Press, 2019), 23-43.

480. Ibbetson, David J. "Law Reporting, Authority and Precedent: The Common Law Paradigm." In *Authorities in Early Modern Law Courts* (Guido Rossi, ed.; Edinburgh: Edinburgh University Press, 2021), 84-97.

481. Ingraham, Patricia Clare. "Losing French: Vernacularity, Nation, and Caxton's English Statutes." In *Caxton's Trace: Studies in the History of English Printing* (William Kuskin, ed.; Notre Dame, IN: University of Notre Dame Press, 2006), 275-298.

482. *An Introductory Survey of the Sources and Literature of Scots Laws*. Hector McKechnie, ed. Edinburgh: Printed for the Stair Society by R. Maclehose & Co., 1936.

483. Ivanenko, V. S. "Private International Law in Russia: The Earliest Work." *Jus Gentium: Journal of International Legal History* 3, no. 1 (Jan. 2018): 245-256.

484. Ives, E. W. "A Lawyer's Library in 1500." *Law Quarterly Review* 85, no. 1 (Jan. 1969): 104-116.

485. Ives, E. W. "The Purpose and Making of the Later Year Books." *Law Quarterly Review* 89, no. 1 (Jan. 1973): 64-86.

486. Ives, E. W. "The Origins of the Later Year Books." In *Legal History Studies 1972: Papers Presented to the Legal History Conference: Aberystwyth, 18-21 July 1972* (Dafydd Jenkins, ed.; Cardiff: University of Wales Press, 1975), 136-151.

487. Izbicki, Thomas M. "Manuscript Works of Bartolus de Saxoferrato in the Vatican Library." *Rivista Internazionale di Diritto Comune* 23 (2012): 147-210.

488. Jäger, Felix. "Framing the Law: Joos de Damhouder and the Legal Iconology of the Grotesque." In *The Art*

of Law: Artistic Representations and Iconography of Law and Justice in Context, from the Middle Ages to the First World War (Stefan Huygebaert *et al.*, eds.; Cham, Switzerland: Springer, 2018), 223-244.

489. Jakab, Éva. "Brissonius in Context: *De formulis et solennibus populi Romani verbis.*" In *Reassessing Legal Humanism and Its Claims: Petere Fontes?* (Paul J. du Plessis & John W. Cairns, eds.; Edinburgh: Edinburgh University Press, 2016), 211-243.

490. James, Eldon R. "The First Printed English Law Book." *American Bar Association Journal* 19, no. 3 (Mar. 1933): 185-187.

491. James, Eldon R. *A List of Legal Treatises Printed in the British Colonies and the American States before 1801.* Cambridge, MA: Harvard University Press, 1934. Reprinted: Union, NJ: Lawbook Exchange, 2002.

492. Jansen, Nils. *The Making of Legal Authority: Non-Legislative Codifications in Historical and Comparative Perspective.* Oxford: Oxford University Press, 2010.

493. Jarvis, Robert M. "John B. West: Founder of the West Publishing Company." *American Journal of Legal History* 50, no. 1 (Jan. 2010): 1-22.

494. Jarvis, Robert M. "A History of the West Nutshells." *Law Library Journal* 114, no. 1 (2022): 31-58.

495. Jenkins, Dafydd. "The Lawbooks of Medieval Wales." In *The Political Context of Law: Proceedings of the Seventh British Legal History Conference, Canterbury 1985* (Richard Eales & David Sullivan, eds.; London: Hambledon Press, 1987), 1-15.

496. Jenkins, Dafydd. "Borrowings in the Welsh Lawbooks." In *Adventures of the Law: Proceedings of the Sixteenth British Legal History Conference, Dublin, 2003* (Paul Brand, *et al.*, eds.; Dublin: Four Courts Press, 2005), 19-39.

497. Jessen, Edward W. "Official Law Reporting in the United States." In *Proceedings of the Second International Symposium on Official Law Reporting, July 30, 2004* (St. Paul, MN: Thomson West, 2004), 28-39.

498. Jimeno Aranguren, Roldán. "The Origins of *Ius commune*: Glosses and Glossaries from the Tenth and Eleventh Centuries." *Glossae: European Journal of Legal History* 14 (2017), 806-817.

499. Johansson, Karl G., & Lena Liepe. "Text and Images in Norwegian and Icelandic Fourteenth-Century Legal Manuscripts." In *The Power of the Book: Medial Approaches to Medieval Nordic Legal Manuscripts* (Lena Rohrbach, ed.; Berlin: Nordeuropa-Institut der Humboldt-Universität, 2014), 129-156.

500. Johnson, Andrew. "The Influences of Nathan Dane on Legal Literature." *American Journal of Legal History* 7, no. 1 (Jan. 1963): 28-50.

501. Johnson, Herbert A. *Imported Eighteenth Century Law Treatises in American Libraries, 1700-1799.* Knoxville, TN: University of Tennessee Press, 1978.

502. Jones, H. Kay. *Butterworths: History of a Publishing House.* London: Butterworths, 1980.

503. Jónsson, Már. "The Size of Medieval Icelandic Legal Manuscripts." In *The Power of the Book: Medial Approaches to Medieval Nordic Legal Manuscripts* (Lena Rohrbach, ed.; Berlin: Nordeuropa-Institut der Humboldt-Universität, 2014), 25-38.

504. Joyce, Craig. "Wheaton v. Peters (33 U.S. [8 Pet.] 591): The Untold Story of the Early Reporters." *Supreme Court Historical Society Yearbook* (1985): 35-92.

505. Joyce, Craig. "The Rise of the Supreme Court Reporter: An Institutional Perspective on Marshall Court Ascendancy." *Michigan Law Review* 83, no. 5 (Mar. 1985): 1291-1391.

506. Joyce, Craig. "The Torch is Passed: In-Chambers Opinions and the Reporter of Decisions in Historical Perspective." In *A Collection of In Chambers Opinions by the Justices of the Supreme Court of the United States* (Cynthia Rapp, comp.; 4 vols.; Washington, DC: Green Bag Press, 2004-2005), 3:vii-xxiii.

507. Joyce, Craig. "A Curious Chapter in the History of Judicature: Wheaton v. Peters and the Rest of the Story (of Copyright in the New Republic)." *Houston Law Review* 42, no. 2 (Summer 2005): 325-392.

508. Jumonville, Florence M. "'The People's Friend, the Tyrant's Foe': Law-Related New Orleans Imprints, 1803-1860." In *A Law Unto Itself? Essays in the New Louisiana Legal History* (Warren M. Billings & Mark F. Fernandez, eds.; Baton Rouge: Louisiana State University Press, 2001), 40-57.

509. Jumonville, Florence M. "'Formerly the Property of a Lawyer' — Books that Shaped Louisiana Law." *Tulane European & Civil Law Forum* 24 (2009): 161-190.

510. Kaiser, Wolfgang. "Justinian and the *Corpus Juris Civilis*." In *The Cambridge Companion to Roman Law* (David Johnston, ed.; Cambridge: Cambridge University Press, 2015), 119-148.

511. Kalm, Gustav. "The Mechanical Art of Rhetoric in an Ordinary Sixteenth Century German Formulary." In *The Art of Law: Artistic Representations and Iconography of Law and Justice in Context, from the Middle Ages to the First World War* (Stefan Huygebaert *et al.*, eds.; Cham, Switzerland: Springer, 2018), 245-272.

512. Kamali, Mohammad Hashim. "Legal Maxims and Other Genres of Literature in Islamic Jurisprudence." *Arab Law Quarterly* 20, no. 1 (Jan. 2006): 77-101.

513. Kantorowicz, Hermann. *Studies in the Glossators of the Roman Law: Newly Discovered Writings of the Twelfth Century.* Cambridge, UK: Cambridge University Press, 1938.

514. Kantorowicz, Hermann. "Note on the Development of the Gloss to the Justinian and the Canon Law." In Beryl Smalley, *The Study of the Bible in the Middle Ages* (Oxford: Clarendon Press, 1941), 36-39.

515. Karachuk, Robert Feikema. "A Workman's Tools: The Law Library of Henry Adams Bullard." *American Journal of Legal History* 42, no. 2 (Apr. 1998): 160-189.

516. Karpuk, Susan. "Cataloging Seventeenth- and Eighteenth-Century German Dissertations: Guidelines and Observations." *Cataloging & Classification Quarterly* 48, no. 4 (2010): 303-314.

517. Katsh, M. Ethan. "Communications Revolutions and Legal Revolutions: The New Media and the Future of Law." *Nova Law Journal* 8, no. 3 (Spring 1984): 631-670.

518. Katz, Farley P. "The Art of Taxation: Joseph Hémard's Illustrated Tax Code." *Tax Lawyer* 60, no. 1 (Fall 2006): 163-176.

519. Katz, W. A. "An Episode in Patronage: Federal Laws Published in Newspapers." *American Journal of Legal History* 10, no. 3 (July 1966): 214-223.

520. Kearley, Timothy G. "A Survey of Medieval European Law and Legal Literature." *Legal Reference Services Quarterly* 3, no. 2 (Summer 1983): 25-66.

521. Kearley, Timothy G. "Justice Fred Blume and the Translation of Justinian's Code." *Law Library Journal* 99, no. 3 (Summer 2007): 525-554.

522. Kearley, Timothy G. "The Creation and Transmission of Justinian's Novels." *Law Library Journal* 102, no. 3 (Summer 2010): 377-397.

523. Kearley, Timothy G. "The Enigma of Samuel Parsons Scott." *Roman Legal Tradition* 10 (2014): 1-37.

524. Kearley, Timothy G. "From Rome to the Restatement: S.P. Scott, Fred Blume, Clyde Pharr, and Roman Law

in Early Twentieth-Century America." *Law Library Journal* 108, no. 1 (Winter 2016): 55-76.

525. Kelly, W. A. *The Library of Lord George Douglas (ca. 1667/8?-1693?): An Early Donation to the Advocates Library*. Cambridge, LP Publications, 1997.

526. Kemp, William. "Where and How to Print the Florentine Pandects: Paris, Basle, Lyons, Venice or Florence?" *Livre - Revue historique* 2019: 1-10.

527. Kennedy, Duncan. "The Structure of Blackstone's Commentaries." *Buffalo Law Review* 28, no. 2 (Spring 1979): 205-382.

528. Kennedy, Kathleen E. "Prosopography of the Book and the Politics of Legal Language in Late Medieval England." *Journal of British Studies* 53, no. 3 (July 2014): 565-587.

529. Kenneth Spencer Research Library. *Civil, Canon and Common: Aspects of Legal History.* Lawrence, KS: Kenneth Spencer Research Library, University of Kansas, 1996.

530. Kenny, Colum. *King's Inns and the Battle of the Books, 1972: Cultural Controversy at a Dublin Library*. Dublin: Four Courts Press, 2002.

531. Kéry, Lotte. *Canonical Collections of the Early Middle Ages (ca. 400-1140): A Bibliographical Guide to the Manuscripts and Literature*. Washington, DC: Catholic University of America Press, 1999.

532. Keynes, Simon. "The Engraved Facsimile by John Pine (1733) of the 'Canterbury' Magna Carta (1215)." In *English Legal History and Its Sources: Essays in Honour of Sir John Baker*, (David Ibbetson *et al.*; eds.; Cambridge, UK: Cambridge University Press, 2019), 223-244.

533. Kirsop, Wallace. "Australian Lawyers and Their Libraries in the Nineteenth Century." *Bulletin (Bibliographical*

Society of Australia and New Zealand) 18, no. 1 (1994): 44-52.

534. Kirsop, Wallace. *Buying Law Books in Nineteenth-Century Melbourne.* Clayton, Vic.: Centre for the Book, Monash University, 2003.

535. Kisch, Guido. "Juridicial Lexicography and the Reception of Roman Law." *Seminar (Jurist)* 2 (1944): 51-81.

536. Knafla, Louis A. "The Law Studies of an Elizabethan Student." *Huntington Library Quarterly* 32, no. 3 (May 1969): 221-240.

537. Korporowicz, Lukacz Jan. "George Harris and the Comparative Legal Background of the First English Translation of Justinian's *Institutes.*" In *Common Law, Civil Law, and Colonial Law: Essays in Comparative Legal History from the Twelfth to the Twentieth Centuries* (William Eves, *et al.*, eds; Cambridge, UK: Cambridge University Press, 2021), 120-139.

538. Krafl, Pavel. "Czech Codifications in the High Middle Ages." In *Honos alit artes: studi per il settantesimo compleanno di Mario Ascheri* (4 vols.; Paola Maffei & Gian Maria Varanini, eds.; Firenze: Firenze University Press, 2014), 3:237-244.

539. Krause, Thomas. "Networking across the North Sea: The Influence of German Civilian Authors on Sir George Mackenzie's *Laws and Customs of Scotland in Matters Criminal.*" *Edinburgh Law Review* 22, no. 3 (Sept. 2018): 368-379.

540. Kreps, Barbara. "Elizabeth Pickering: The First Woman to Print Law Books in England and Relations within the Community of Tudor London's Printers and Lawyers." *Renaissance Quarterly* 56, no. 4 (Winter 2003): 1053-1088.

541. Kuskowski, Ada Maria. *Vernacular Law: Writing and the Reinvention of Customary Law in Medieval France.* Cambridge, UK: Cambridge University Press, 2022.

542. Kuttner, Stephan. "Raymond of Penafort as Editor: The 'Decretales' and 'Constitutiones' of Gregory IX." *Bulletin of Medieval Canon Law* 12 (1982): 65-80.

543. L'Engle, Susan, & Robert Gibbs. *Illuminating the Law: Legal Manuscripts in Cambridge Collections.* London: H. Miller, 2001.

544. L'Engle, Susan. "Trends in Bolognese Legal Illustration: The Early Trecento." In *Juristische Buchproduktion im Mittelalter* (Vincenzo Colli, ed.; Frankfurt am Main: Vittorio Klostermann, 2002), 219-244.

545. L'Engle, Susan. "The Pro-Active Reader: Learning to Learn the Law." In *Medieval Manuscripts, Their Makers and Users: A Special Issue of Viator in Honor of Richard and Mary Rouse* (Turnhout, Belgium: Brepols, 2011), 51-75.

546. L'Engle, Susan, & Ariane Bergeron-Foote. *Law (Primer 3).* New York: Les Enluminures, 2014.

547. Laeuchli, Ann Jordan. *A Bibliographical Catalog of William Blackstone.* Buffalo, N.Y.: Published for Yale Law Library by William S. Hein & Co., 2015.

548. Lancashire, Ian. "Law and Early Modern English Lexicons." In *Selected Proceedings of the 2005 Symposium on New Approaches in English Historical Lexis* (R. W. McConchie, *et al.*, eds.; Somerville, MA: Cascadilla Proceedings Project, 2006), 8-23. http://www.lingref.com/cpp/hel-lex/2005/paper1342.pdf

549. Landau, Peter. "Gratian and the Decretum Gratiani." In *The History of Medieval Canon Law in the Classical Period, 1140-1234: From Gratian to the Decretals of Pope Gregory IX* (Wilfried Hartmann & Kenneth Pennington, eds.; Washington, DC: Catholic University of America Press, 2008), 22-54.

550. Langbein, John H. "Chancellor Kent and the History of Legal Literature." *Columbia Law Review* 93, no. 3 (Apr. 1993): 547-594.

551. LaPiana, William P. "Dusty Books and Living History: Why All Those Old State Reports Really Matter." *Law Library Journal* 81, no. 1 (Winter 1989): 33-39.

552. Lathrop, Olive C. "History of Michigan Law Libraries and Their Relation to General Libraries in Michigan." *Law Library Journal* 16, no. 3 (Oct. 1923): 15-22.

553. *Law and the Christian Tradition in Italy: The Legacy of the Great Jurists*. Rafael Domingo & Orazio Condorelli, eds. London; New York: Routledge, 2021.

554. Law Library of Congress. *Library of Congress Law Library: An Illustrated Guide*. Washington, D.C.: Library of Congress, 2005.

555. Lawson, F. H. "Institutes." In *Festschrift für Imre Zajtay / Mélanges en l'honneur d'Imre Zajtay* (Tübingen: J. C. B. Mohr, 1982), 333-355.

556. Le Patourel, John. "The Authorship of the Grand Coutumier de Normandie." *English Historical Review* 56, no. 222 (Apr. 1941): 292-300.

557. Lepsius, Susanne. "Editing Legal Texts from the Late Middle Ages." In *Textual Cultures of Medieval Italy* (William Robins, ed.; Toronto: University of Toronto Press, 2011), 295-324.

558. Library of Congress. *The Canon Law Collection of the Library of Congress: A General Bibliography with Selective Annotations*. Washington, DC: G.P.O., 1981. Reprinted: Clark, N.J.: Lawbook Exchange, 2003.

559. Liendo Tagle, Fernando. "A Spanish Legal Journal Defining the Centre and the Periphery: *Revista de Legislación y Jurisprudencia de Ultramar* (1877-1878)." *Journal on European History of Law* 12, no. 2 (2021): 79-85.

560. Lind, Douglas W. "An Economic Analysis of Early Casebook Publishing." *Law Library Journal* 96, no. 1 (Winter 2004): 95-126.

561. Lind, Douglas W. *Lincoln's Suspension of Habeas Corpus: The Pamphlet Literature and Congressional Debate*. Buffalo, NY: William S. Hein & Co., 2012.

562. Lind, Douglas W. "An Analysis of the Joseph Story Collection at Southern Illinois University Law Library." *Unbound: A Review of Legal History and Rare Books* 8 (2015): 51-60. https://www.aallnet.org/lhrbsis/resources-publications/unbound/

563. Lind, Douglas W., & Alicia G. Jones. "The Constitutional Conventions of Illinois: An Annotated Bibliography." *Southern Illinois University Law Journal* 40, no. 2 (Winter 2016): 221-270.

564. Lind, Douglas W. *Dred Scott v. Sandford: Opinions and Contemporary Commentary, with a Bibliographic Essay.* Getzville, NY: William S. Hein & Co., 2017.

565. Lind, Douglas W. "A Bibliography of Littleton's *Tenures* as an Archetype for the Study of Early English Legal Printing." *Legal Reference Services Quarterly* 37, no. 1 (2018): 38-74.

566. Lind, Douglas W. *Bibliography of American Law School Casebooks, 1870-2018*. 2nd ed. Buffalo, NY: William S. Hein & Co., 2020.

567. Little, Eleanor N. "The Acquisition of the Dunn Collection of Early English Law Books." *Harvard Law School Bulletin* 7, no. 3 (Dec. 1955): 10-11.

568. Lobban, Michael. "The English Legal Treatise and English Law in the Eighteenth Century." In *Auctoritates, xenia R.C. van Caenegem oblata: Law Making and Its Authors* (Serge Dauchy *et al.*, eds.; Brussels: Wetenschappelijk Comité voor Rechtsgeschiedenis, Koninklijke Academie voor Wetenschappen, Letteren en Schone Kunsten van België, 1997), 69-88.

569. Lobban, Michael. "Rationalising the Common Law: Blackstone and His Predecessors." In *Re-interpreting Blackstone's Commentaries: A Seminal Text in National*

and International Contexts (Wilfrid Prest, ed.; Oxford, UK: Hart Publishing, 2014), 1-22.

570. Longa, Ernesto. "A History of America's First Jim Crow Law School Library and Staff." *Connecticut Public Interest Law Journal* 7, no. 1 (Fall 2007): 77-104.

571. Loretelli, Rosamaria. "The First English Translation of Cesare Beccaria's *On Crimes and Punishments*: Uncovering the Editorial and Political Contexts." *Diciottesimo Secolo* 2 (2017): 1-22. https://doi.org/10.13128/ds-20618

572. Loretelli, Rosamaria. "The First English Translation of *Dei delitti e delle pene*: A Question of Sources and Modifications." *Diciottesimo Secolo* 4 (2019): 95-106. https://doi.org/10.13128/ds-25442

573. Lucas, Peter J. "Printing Anglo-Saxon in Holland and John Selden's *Mare Clausum seu de Dominio Maris*." *Quaerendo* 31, no. 2 (Jan. 2001): 120-136.

574. Luig, Klaus. "The Institutes of National Law in the Seventeenth and Eighteenth Centuries." *Juridical Review* 17 (1972), 193-226.

575. Luther, Peter. "The Year Books." *Law Librarian* 13, no. 2 (Aug. 1982): 19-22.

576. Lynch, Michael J. "Citators in the Early Twentieth Century - Not Just Shepard's." *Legal Reference Services Quarterly* 16, no. 3 (1998): 5-22.

577. Macalister-Smith, Peter, & Joachim Schwietzke. "Literature and Documentary Sources Relating to the History of Public International Law: An Annotated Bibliographical Survey." *Journal of the History of International Law* 1, no. 2 (Feb. 1999): 136-212.

578. Macalister-Smith, Peter, & Joachim Schwietzke. "Bibliography of the Textbooks and Comprehensive Treatises on Positive International Law of the 19th Century." *Journal of the History of International Law* 3, no. 1 (2001): 75-142.

579. Macalister-Smith, Peter, & Joachim Schwietzke. "Jus Gentium and Globally-Conceived General Treaty Collections." *Jus Gentium: Journal of International Legal History* 1, no. 1 (Jan. 2016): 235-316.

580. Macalister-Smith, Peter, & Joachim Schwietzke. "Publication of Treaty Collections Relating to Spain and Portugal in Historical Perspective: A Baseline Compilation." *Jus Gentium: Journal of International Legal History* 1, no. 2 (July 2016): 639-694.

581. Macalister-Smith, Peter, & Joachim Schwietzke. "Latin American Treaty Collections and International Law Textbooks: from Independence to World War One." *Jus Gentium: Journal of International Legal History* 4, no. 1 (Jan. 2019): 207-284.

582. Machado Cabral, Gustavo César. "Foreign Law and Circulation of Ideas in the Early Modern Age: Analyzing an 'allegatio' of Manuel Álvares Pegas on *maioratus*." *Forum Historiae Iuris* (2019). https://forhistiur.de/2018-12-cabral

583. Machado Cabral, Gustavo César." Legal Authorities in the Making of Portuguese Private Law: Emphytheusis and Majorat in Practical Literature." In *Authorities in Early Modern Law Courts* (Guido Rossi, ed.; Edinburgh: Edinburgh University Press, 2021), 98-121.

584. Maclean, Ian. *Interpretation and Meaning in the Renaissance: The Case of Law.* Cambridge, UK: Cambridge University Press, 2005.

585. Maclean, Ian. "Alberico Gentili, His Publishers, and the Vagaries of the Book Trade Between England and Germany, 1580-1614." In Ian Maclean, *Learning the Market Place: Essays in the History of the Early Modern Book* (Leiden: Brill, 2009), 291-337.

586. Maclean, Ian. "The Thesauruses of Otto and Meerman as Publishing Enterprises: Legal Humanism in its Last Phase, 1725-1780." In *Reassessing Legal Humanism and Its Claims: Petere Fontes?* (Paul J. du Plessis &

John W. Cairns, eds.; Edinburgh: Edinburgh University Press, 2016), 299-347.

587. Macnair, Michael. "Sir Jeffrey Gilbert and His Treatises." *Journal of Legal History* 15, no. 3 (Dec. 1994): 252-268.

588. Macnair, Michael. "The Nature and Function of the Early Chancery Reports." In *Law Reporting in Britain* (Chantal Stebbings, ed.; London: Hambledon Press, 1995), 123-132.

589. Maffei, Domenico. "Manuscripts and Legal Publishers in the Early Sixteenth Century (Notes and Suggestions)." In *Proceedings of the Sixth International Congress of Medieval Canon Law* (Stephan Kuttner & Kenneth Penington, eds.; Città del Vaticano: Biblioteca Apostolica Vaticana, 1985), 49-54.

590. Manchester, A. H. *Sources of English Legal History: Law, History and Society in England and Wales, 1750-1950*. London: Butterworths, 1984.

591. Manuwald, Henrike. "Pictorial Narrative in Legal Manuscripts? The Sachsenspiegel Manuscript in Wolfenbuttel." *Word & Image* 23, no. 3 (July-Sept. 2007): 275-289.

592. Manuwald, Henrike. "Book History." In *The Oxford Handbook of Law and Humanities* (Simon Stern *et al.*, eds.; New York: Oxford University Press, 2020), 65-83.

593. Margadant S., Guillermo Floris. *The Illustrations of the Sachsenspiegel: A Medieval German Law Book*. Austin, Tex.: Jamail Center for Legal Research, The University of Texas School of Law, 2000.

594. Marke, Julius, J., ed. *A Catalogue of the Law Collection at New York University: With Selected Annotations*. New York: Law Center of New York University, 1953. Reprinted: Union, NJ: Law Book Exchange, 1999.

595. Marke, Julius J. "The N.Y.U. Law Library Catalogue Revisited." *Legal Reference Services Quarterly* 9, no. 1-2 (1989): 11-32.

148

596. Martin, Jill E. "'A Year and a Spring of My Existence': Felix S. Cohen and the Handbook of Federal Indian Law." *Western Legal History* 8, no. 1 (Winter/Spring 1995): 35-60.

597. Martines, Lauro. "The Career and Library of a 15th-Century Lawyer (Bartolus of Sassoferrato's Grandson)." *Annali di storia del diritto* 3-4 (1959-1960): 323-332.

598. Martinez, Cristina S. "Blackstone as Draughtsman: Picturing the Law." In *Re-interpreting Blackstone's Commentaries: A Seminal Text in National and International Contexts* (Wilfrid Prest, ed.; Oxford, UK: Hart Publishing, 2014), 31-58.

599. Martins, Ryan, & Michael Widener. *Learning the Law: The Book in Early Legal Education.* New Haven: Lillian Goldman Law Library, Yale Law School, 2018.

600. Marvin, William W. *West Publishing Co.: Origin, Growth, Leadership.* St. Paul, MN: West, 1969.

601. Matetsky, Ira Brad. "The History of Publication of U.S. Supreme Court Justices' In-Chambers Opinions." *Journal of Law* 6, no. 1 (2016): 19-31.

602. Matthews, Elizabeth W. *Seventeenth Century English Law Reports in Folio: Description of Selected Imprints.* Buffalo, NY: W. S. Hein, 1986.

603. Matthews, Nancy L. *William Sheppard, Cromwell's Law Reformer.* Cambridge, UK: Cambridge University Press, 1984.

604. Maxwell, M. W. "The Development of Law Publishing." In *Sweet and Maxwell: Then and Now: 1799-1974* (J. Burke & P. Allsop, eds.; London: Sweet & Maxwell, 1974), 121-136.

605. Maxwell, W. Harold, & C. R. Brown. *A Complete List of British and Colonial Law Reports and Legal Periodicals, with a Check List of Canadian Statutes: Arranged in Alphabetical and in Chronological Order*

with Bibliographical Notes. 3rd ed. Toronto: Carswell, 1937. Reprinted: Clark, NJ: Lawbook Exchange, 1995.

606. Mazor, Lester J. "Historic Trials: The Place of Persons in the Order of Things." *Law Library Journal* 69, no. 4 (Nov. 1976): 453-455.

607. McCamic, Charles. "The First Edition of Blackstone's Commentaries." *West Virginia Law Quarterly & The Bar* 33, no. 3 (Apr. 1927): 287-297.

608. McDade, Thomas M. "Gallows Literature of the Streets." *The New Colophon: A Book-Collector's Miscellany* 3 (1950): 120-127.

609. McDade, Thomas M. "Lurid Literature of the Last Century: The Publications of E. E. Barclay." *Pennsylvania Magazine of History & Biography* 80, no. 4 (Oct.1956): 452-464.

610. McDade, Thomas M. *The Annals of Murder: A Bibliography of Books and Pamphlets on American Murders from Colonial Times to 1900.* Norman, OK: University of Oklahoma Press, 1961.

611. McDade, Thomas M. "The 'Corpse' in the Library: A Brief Note on American Trial Publishing." *American Book Collector* 15, no. 1 (Sept. 1964): 8-12.

612. McDowell, Gary L. "The Politics of Meaning: Law Dictionaries and the Liberal Tradition of Interpretation." *American Journal of Legal History* 44, no. 3 (July 2000): 257-283.

613. McGerr, Rosemarie. "A Statute Book and Lancastrian Mirror for Princes: The Yale Law School Manuscript of the Nova Statuta Angliae." *Textual Cultures: Text, Contexts, Interpretation* 1, no. 2 (2006): 6-59.

614. McGerr, Rosemarie. *A Lancastrian Mirror for Princes: The Yale Law School New Statutes of England.* Bloomington: Indiana University Press, 2011.

615. McGlynn, Margaret. "Idiosyncratic Books and Common Learning: Readings on Statutes at the Inns of Court." In

The Oxford Handbook of English Law and Literature, 1500-1700 (Lorna Hutson, ed.; Oxford; New York: Oxford University Press, 2017), 41-60.

616. McIlvenna, Una, Siv Gøril Brandtzæg, & Juan Gomis. "Singing the News of Punishment: The Execution Ballad in Europe, 1550-1900." *Quaerendo* 51, nos. 1-2 (Dec. 2021): 123-159.

617. McInnis, L. R. "Michael Dalton: The Training of the Early Modern Justice of the Peace and the Cromwellian Reforms." In *Learning the Law: Teaching and the Transmission of Law in England, 1150-1900* (Jonathan Bush & Alain A. Wijffels, eds.; London: Hambledon Press, 1999), 255-272.

618. McKitterick, Rosamond. "Some Carolingian Law Books and their Function." In *Authority and Power: Studies on Medieval Law and Government Presented to Walter Ullman on his 70th Birthday* (Peter Linehan & Brian Tierney, eds.; Cambridge: Cambridge University Press, 1980), 13-27.

619. McKnight, Joseph W. "Law Books on the Hispanic Frontier." In *Spanish and Mexican Land Grants and the Law* (Malcolm Ebright, ed.; Manhattan, KS: Sunflower University Press, 1989), 74-84.

620. McSweeney, Thomas J., & Michéle K. Spike. "The Significance of the Corpus Juris Civilis: Matilda of Canossa and the Revival of Roman Law." In *Matilda of Canossa & the Origins of the Renaissance: An Exhibition in Honor of the 900th Anniversary of Her Death* (Williamsburg, VA: Muscarelle Museum of Art at the College of William & Mary, 2015), 21-29.

621. McSweeney, Thomas J. "Creating a Literature for the King's Courts in the Later Thirteenth Century: Hengham Magna, Fet Asaver, and Bracton." *Journal of Legal History* 37, no. 1 (Apr. 2016): 41-71.

622. McSweeney, Thomas J. "Fiction in the Code: Reading Legislation as Literature." *Georgia State University Law Review* 34, no. 3 (Spring 2018): 581-629.

623. McSweeney, Thomas J. "Those Things Which Are Written in Romance: Language and Law Teaching in Thirteenth-Century England." *American Journal of Legal History* 62, no. 4 (Dec. 2022): 285-304.

624. Mead, Robert A., & Michael H. Hoeflich. "Lawyers and Law Books in Nineteenth-Century Kansas." *University of Kansas Law Review* 50, no. 5 (June 2002): 1051-1074.

625. Mead, Robert A. "A Eulogy for New Mexico Reports: The Evolution of Appellate Publication from 1846 to 2012." *New Mexico Law Review* 42, no. 2 (Summer 2012): 417-470.

626. Meador, Daniel J., comp. *Mr. Justice Black and His Books*. Charlottesville, VA: University Press of Virginia, 1974.

627. Meehan, Michael. "Blackstone's *Commentaries*: England's Legal Georgic?" In *Re-interpreting Blackstone's Commentaries: A Seminal Text in National and International Contexts* (Wilfrid Prest, ed.; Oxford, UK: Hart Publishing, 2014), 59-69.

628. Mellinkoff, David. "The Myth of Precision and the Law Dictionary." *UCLA Law Review* 31, no. 2 (Dec. 1983): 423-442.

629. Melnikas, Anthony. *The Corpus of the Miniatures in the Manuscripts of Decretum Gratiani*. 3 vols. Rome: Studia Gratiana, 1975.

630. Mersky, Roy M., *et al.* "Bicentennial History of American Law Libraries." *Law Library Journal* 69, no. 4 (Nov. 1976): 528-553.

631. Mersky, Roy M. "The Evolution and Impact of Legal Dictionaries." *Legal Reference Services Quarterly* 23, no. 1 (2004): 19-35.

632. Metzmeier, Kurt X. "Blazing Trails in a New Kentucky Wilderness: Early Kentucky Case Law Digests." *Law Library Journal* 93, no. 1 (Winter 2001): 93-108.

633. Metzmeier, Kurt X. "James Hughes: Kentucky's First Nominative Reporter." *Unbound: An Annual Review of Legal History and Rare Books* 1 (2008): 25-31. https://www.aallnet.org/lhrbsis/resources-publications/unbound/

634. Metzmeier, Kurt X., & Peter Scott Campbell. "Nursery of a Supreme Court Justice: The Library of James Harlan of Kentucky, Father of John Marshall Harlan." *Law Library Journal* 100, no. 4 (Fall 2008): 639-674.

635. Metzmeier, Kurt X. *Writing the Legal Record: Law Reporters in Nineteenth-Century Kentucky.* Lexington, KY: University Press of Kentucky, 2017.

636. Meyer, Christopher H. F. "Putting Roman and Canon Law in a Nutshell: Developments in the Epitomisation of Legal Texts between Late Antiquity and the Early Modern Period." In *Knowledge of the* Pragmatici: *Legal and Moral Theological Literature and the Formation of Early Modern Ibero-America* (Thomas Duve & Otto Danwerth, eds.; Leiden: Brill Nijhoff, 2020), 40-88.

637. Mikuła, Maciej. "*Iura Scripta* and *Operae iurisperitorum* in Municipal Courts of the Kingdom of Poland (Sixteenth to Eighteenth Centuries)." In *Authorities in Early Modern Law Courts* (Guido Rossi, ed.; Edinburgh: Edinburgh University Press, 2021), 122-136.

638. Milsom, S. F. C. "The Nature of Blackstone's Achievement." *Oxford Journal of Legal Studies* 1, no. 1 (Spring 1981): 1-12.

639. Minot, Martin Jordan. "The Irrelevance of Blackstone: Rethinking the Eighteenth-Century Importance of the *Commentaries.*" *Virginia Law Review* 104, no. 7 (Nov. 2018): 1359-1397.

640. Mirow, Matthew C. "The Ascent of the Readings: Some Evidence from Readings on Wills." In *Learning the Law: Teaching and the Transmission of Law in England, 1150-1900* (Jonathan Bush & Alain A. Wijffels, eds.; London: Hambledon Press, 1999), 227-254.

641. Mirow, Matthew C. "Pre-constitutional Law and Constitutions: Spanish Colonial Law and the Constitution of Cádiz." *Washington University Global Studies Law Review* 12, no. 2 (2013): 313-337.

642. Mirow, Matthew C. *Latin American Constitutions: The Constitution of Cádiz and Its Legacy in Spanish America.* New York: Cambridge University Press, 2015.

643. Modéer, Kjell Å. *Hugo Grotius and Lund.* Lund: Bloms Boktryckeri AB, 1987.

644. Modéer, Kjell Å. "The Law Journal Editors Carl and Gustavus Schmidt: Two Swedish Lawyers and Brothers as Law Journal Pioneers in the 19th Century." *Civil Law Commentaries* 3 (Summer 2011): 1-11.

645. Modéer, Kjell Å. "K. J. A. Mittermaier and the Schmidt Brothers, Carl and Gustavus." *Journal of Civil Law Studies* 8, no. 2 (2015), 409-441.

646. Monballyu, Jos. "Joos de Damhouder, an Internationally Influential Jurist from Bruges." In *The Art of Law: Three Centuries of Justice Depicted* (Stefan Huygebaert *et al.*, eds.; Tielt: Lannoo, 2018), 106-119.

647. Moran, C. G. *The Heralds of the Law.* London: Stevens, 1948.

648. Moreland, John L. "Organized for Service: The Hicks Classification System and the Evolution of Law School Curriculum." *Law Library Journal* 114, no. 3 (2022): 305-317.

649. Moreton, C. E. "The 'Library' of a Late-Fifteenth-Century Lawyer." *The Library: Transactions of the Bibliographical Society*, 6th series 13, no. 4 (Dec. 1991): 338-346.

650. Morin, Michael. "Blackstone and the Birth of Quebec's Distinct Legal Culture 1765-1867." In *Re-interpreting Blackstone's Commentaries: A Seminal Text in National and International Contexts* (Wilfrid Prest, ed.; Oxford, UK: Hart Publishing, 2014), 105-124.

651. Muller, Wolfgang P. "The Recovery of Justinian's Digest in the Middle Ages." *Bulletin of Medieval Canon Law* 20 (1990): 1-30.

652. Mulligan, Christina, *et al.* "Founding-Era Translations of the U.S. Constitution." *Constitutional Commentary* 31, no. 1 (Spring 2016): 1-54.

653. Murray, A. L. "Sinclair's Practicks." In *Law-Making and Law-Makers in British History: Papers Presented to the Edinburgh Legal History Conference, 1977* (Alan Harding, ed.; London: Royal Historical Society, 1980), 90-104.

654. Musson, Anthony. "Law and Text: The Impact on Legal Authority and Judicial Accessibility in the Late Middle Ages." In *The Uses of Script and Print, 1300-1700* (Julia Crick & Alexandra Walsham, eds.; Cambridge, UK: Cambridge University Press, 2004), 95-115.

655. Musson, Anthony. "Sir Edward Coke and his *Institutes of the Laws of England*: An Exercise in Legal History?" *Archives: The Journal of the British Records Association* 31, no. 115 (Dec. 2006): 95-107.

656. Musson, Anthony. "Ruling 'Virtually'? Royal Images in Medieval English Law Books." In *Every Inch a King: Comparative Studies on Kings and Kingship in the Ancient and Medieval Worlds* (Lynette Mitchell & Charles Melville, eds.; Leiden: Brill, 2013), 151-171.

657. Musson, Anthony. "Seeing Justice: The Visual Culture of the Law and Lawyers." *Miscellanea Mediaevalia* 38 (2014): 711-721.

658. Musson, Anthony. "Illuminating Magna Carta: Images of Law and Authority in Medieval Statute Books." In

Challenges to Authority and the Recognition of Rights: From Magna Carta to Modernity (Catharine MacMillan & Charlotte Smith, eds.; Cambridge, UK: Cambridge University Press, 2018), 70-96.

659. Musson, Anthony. "Illuminated English Law Books." *Clio@Themis* 21 (2021). https://doi.org/10.35562/ cliothemis.1808

660. Nadelmann, Kurt H. "Apropos of Translations (Federalist, Kent, Story)." *American Journal of Comparative Law* 8, no. 2 (Spring 1959), 204-214.

661. Nann, John B., & Morris L. Cohen. *The Yale Law School Guide to Research in American Legal History.* New Haven: Yale University Press, 2018.

662. Nellen, Henk. "On the Occasion of the Acquisition of the First Edition of *De iure belli ac pacis* by the Peace Palace Library." *Grotiana* 33, no. 1 (Jan. 2012): 1-21. Also published, with illustrations, as *Grotius's Memory Honored: On the Acquisition of the First Edition of "De iure belli ac pacis" by the Peace Palace Library* (The Hague: Peace Palace Library, 2012).

663. Nilsén, Per. "The Influence of Foreign Legal Literature in the Works and Teachings of David Nehrman Ehrenstråle." *Clio@Themis* 2 (2009). https://doi. org/10.35562/cliothemis.1791

664. Nova, Rodolfo de. "The First American Book on Conflict of Laws." *American Journal of Legal History* 8, no. 2 (Apr. 1964): 136-156.

665. O'Brien, Bruce R. "An English Book of Laws from the Time of Glanvill." In *Laws, Lawyers, and Texts: Studies in Medieval Legal History in Honour of Paul Brand* (Susanne Jenks *et al.*, eds.; Leiden: Brill, 2012), 51-67.

666. O'Connor, Sharon Hamby, & Mary Sarah Bilder. "Appeals to the Privy Council before American Independence: An Annotated Digital Catalogue." *Law Library Journal* 104, no. 1 (Winter 2012): 83-97.

667. O'Higgins, Paul. *A Bibliography of Irish Trials and Other Legal Proceedings.* Abingdon, UK: Professional Books, 1986.

668. O'Higgins, Paul. "Law Printing in Eighteenth Century Ireland." *Law Librarian* 17, no. 3 (Dec. 1986): 93-94.

669. O'Higgins, Paul. "An *Essai* on Puzzles in Irish Legal Bibliography." *Irish Jurist* 36 (2001): 214-226.

670. O'Sullivan, Dominic. "The Nominate Reports (1535-1865)." *Queensland Legal Yearbook 2014*, 90-112. https://archive.sclqld.org.au/sclpub/queensland-legal-yearbook/2014/queensland-legal-yearbook-2014.pdf

671. O'Sullivan, Richard. *Edmund Plowden, 1518-1585: Autumn Reading Given in the Presence of Her Majesty Queen Elizabeth, the Queen Mother at the Middle Temple Hall on 12 November 1952.* Cambridge, UK: University Press, 1952.

672. Ogden, Patti J. "'Mastering the Lawless Science of Our Law': A Story of Legal Citation Indexes." *Law Library Journal* 85, no. 1 (Winter 1993): 1-48.

673. Oldham, James. "Eighteenth-Century Judges' Notes: How They Explain, Correct and Enhance the Reports." *American Journal of Legal History* 31, no. 1 (Jan. 1987): 9-42.

674. Oldham, James. "Law Reporting in the London Newspapers, 1756-1786." *American Journal of Legal History* 31, no. 3 (July 1987): 177-206.

675. Oldham, James. "The Indispensability of Manuscript Case Notes to Eighteenth-Century Barristers and Judges." In *Making Legal History: Approaches and Methodologies* (A. Musson & C. Stebbings, eds.; Cambridge: Cambridge University Press 2012), 30-52.

676. Orth, John V. "Blackstone's Ghost: Law and Legal Education in North Carolina." In *Re-interpreting Blackstone's Commentaries: A Seminal Text in National*

and International Contexts (Wilfrid Prest, ed.; Oxford, UK: Hart Publishing, 2014), 125-143.

677. Osborough, W. N. "In Praise of Law Books." *Irish Jurist* 21, no. 2 (Winter 1986): 326-357.

678. Osborough, W. N. "Puzzles from Irish Law Reporting History." In *The Life of the Law: Proceedings of the Tenth British Legal History Conference, Oxford 1991* (Peter Birks, ed.; London: Hambledon Press, 1993), 89-111. Reprinted: W. N. Osborough, *Studies in Irish Legal History* (Dublin: Four Courts Press, 1999), 193-212.

679. Osborough, W. N. "The History of Irish Legal Publishing: A Challenge Unmet." *Irish Jurist* 35 (2000): 355-374.

680. Osler, Douglas J. "The Compilation of Justinian's Digest." *Zeitschrift der Savigny-Stiftung für Rechtsgeschichte: Romanistische Abteilung* 102 (1985): 129-184.

681. Osler, Douglas J. "Turning the Title-Page." *Rechtshistorisches Journal* 6 (1987): 173-182.

682. Osler, Douglas J. "Towards a Legal-Historical Bibliography: A Census of 16th Century Legal Imprints." *Ius Commune* 15 (1988): 231-242.

683. Osler, Douglas J. "Dies diem docet." *Ius Commune* 18 (1991): 207-224.

684. Osler, Douglas J. "Developments in the Text of Alciatus' *Dispunctiones*." *Ius Commune* 19 (1992): 219-235.

685. Osler, Douglas J. "Magna Jurisprudentiae Injuria: Cornelius van Bynkershoek on Early Legal Humanist Philology." *Ius Commune* 19 (1992): 61-79.

686. Osler, Douglas J. "Vestigia doctorum virorum: Tracking the Legal Humanists' Manuscripts." *Subseciva Groningana: Studies in Roman and Byzantine Law* 5 (1992), 77-94.

687. Osler, Douglas J. "Scoto-Dutch Law Books of the Seventeenth and Eighteenth Centuries." In *Lines of Contact: Proceedings of the Second Conference*

158

of Belgian, British, Irish and Dutch Historians of Universities Held at St. Anne's College, Oxford, 15-17 September 1989 (John M. Fletcher & Hilde de Ridder-Symoens, eds.; Gent: Universiteit Gent, 1994), 57-74.

688. Osler, Douglas J. "Text and Technology." *Rechtshistorisches Journal* 14 (1995): 309-331.

689. Osler, Douglas J. *Catalogue of Books Printed in Spain, Portugal and the Southern and Northern Netherlands from the Beginning of Printing to 1800 in the Library of the Max-Planck-Institut* für *Europäische Rechtsgeschichte.* Frankfurt am Main. Frankfurt: V. Klostermann, 2000.

690. Osler, Douglas J. *Catalogue of Books Printed on the Continent of Europe from the Beginning of Printing to 1600 in the Library of the Max-Planck- Institut* für *Europäische Rechtsgeschichte.* Frankfurt am Main. Frankfurt: V. Klostermann, 2000.

691. Osler, Douglas J. "Images of Legal Humanism." *Surfaces* 9 (2001). https://doi.org/10.7202/1065066ar

692. Osler, Douglas J. *Edoardo Volterra, 1904-1984: A Catalogue of the Early Printed Books in His Library, Now in the Ecole Française de Rome.* Frankfurt am Main: Vittorio Klostermann, 2006.

693. Osler, Douglas J. "The Fantasy Men." *Rechtsgeschichte (Rg)* 10 (2007): 169-192.

694. Osler, Douglas J. "A Survey of the Roman-Dutch Law." In *Iuris historia: liber amicorum Gero Dolezalek* (Vincenzo Colli & Emanuele Conte, eds.; Berkeley, CA: Robbins Collection Publications, 2008), 405-422.

695. Osler, Douglas J. *Jurisprudence of the Baroque: A Census of Seventeenth Century Italian Legal Imprints.* 3 vols. Frankfurt am Main: Vittorio Klostermann, 2009.

696. Osler, Douglas J. *Catalogue of Books Printed Before 1801 in the Legal Historical Section of the Biblioteca di Scienze Sociali dell'Università degli Studi di Firenze.* 2 vols. Firenze: Firenze University Press, 2014.

697. Osler, Douglas. "Humanist Philology and the Text of Justinian's Digest." In *Reassessing Legal Humanism and its Claims: Petere Fontes?* (Paul J. du Plessis & John W. Cairns, eds.; Edinburgh: Edinburgh University Press, 2016), 41-56.

698. Osler, Douglas J. "The Restless Mind and the Living Text: The First Edition of Grotius's *De iure belli ac pacis*." *Grotiana* 37, no. 1 (Dec. 2016): 1-15.

699. Ossipow, William, & Dominik Gerber. "The Reception of Vattel's Law of Nations in the American Colonies: From James Otis and John Adams to the Declaration of Independence." *American Journal of Legal History* 57, no. 4 (Dec. 2017): 521-555.

700. Padovani, Andrea. "The 'Additiones et Apostillae super secunda parte Infortiati' of Cinus de Pistoia." In *The Two Laws: Studies in Medieval History Dedicated to Stephan Kuttner* (Laurent Mayali & Stephanie A.J. Tibbets, eds.; Washington: The Catholic University of America, 1990), 152-165.

701. Padwa, David J. "On the English Translation of John Selden's Mare Clausum." *American Journal of International Law* 54, no. 1 (Jan. 1960): 156-159.

702. Palmer, Vernon Valentine. *The Lost Translators of 1808 and the Birth of Civil Law in Louisiana*. Athens, Ga.: University of Georgia Press, 2021.

703. Pantzer, Katherine F. "Printing the English Statutes, 1484-1640: Some Historical Implications." In *Books and Society in History: Papers of the Association of College and Research Libraries Rare Books and Manuscripts Preconference, 24-28 June, 1980, Boston, Massachusetts* (Kenneth E. Carpenter, ed.; New York: R.R. Bowker, 1983), 69-114.

704. Panzanelli Fratoni, Maria Alessandra. "The Cartolari Family from Perugia: From Paper Sellers to Publishing House." In *Lux Librorum: Essays on Books and History*

for Chris Coppens (Goran Proot, *et al.*, eds.; Mechelen: Flanders Book Historical Society, 2018), 1-15.

705. Panzanelli Fratoni, Maria Alessandra. "Building an Up-to-date Library: Prospero Podiani's Use of Booksellers' Catalogues, with Special Reference to Law Books." *JLIS.it* 9, no. 2 (May 2018): 74-113. http://dx.doi. org/10.4403/jlis.it-12463

706. Panzanelli Fratoni, Maria Alessandra. "Printing the Law in the 15th Century with a Focus on *Corpus iuris civilis* and the Works of Bartolus de Saxoferrato." In *Printing R-Evolution and Society 1450-1500: Fifty Years that Changed Europe* (Cristina Dondi, ed.; Venezia: Edizioni Ca' Foscari, 2020), 67-197.

707. Parise, Agustín. "The Place of the Louisiana Civil Code in the Hispanic Civil Codifications: The Comments to the Spanish Civil Code Project of 1851." *Louisiana Law Review* 68, no. 3 (Spring 2008): 823-929.

708. Parise, Agustín. Book Review. *Journal of Civil Law Studies* 2 (2009): 183-193. [Review essay of Gustavus Schmidt, *The Civil Law of Spain and Mexico*, (Buffalo, NY: William S. Hein & Co., 2008).]

709. Parise, Agustín. "A Constant Give and Take: Tracing Legal Borrowings in the Louisiana Civil Law Experience." *Seton Hall Legislative Journal* 35, no. 1 (2010): 1-35.

710. Parise, Agustín. "Libraries of Civil Codes as Mirrors of Normative Transfers from Europe to the Americas: The Experiences of Lorimier in Quebec (1871-1890) and Varela in Argentina (1873-1875)." In *Entanglements in Legal History: Conceptual Approaches* (Thomas Duve, ed.; Frankfurt am Main: Max Planck Institute for European Legal History, 2014), 315-384.

711. Parise, Agustín. "Translators' Preface to the Laws of Las Siete Partidas which are Still in Force in the State of Louisiana." *Journal of Civil Law Studies* 7, no. 1 (Oct. 2014): 311-353.

712. Parise, Agustín. "A Translator's Toolbox: The Law, Moreau-Lislet's Library, and the Presence of Multilingual Dictionaries in Nineteenth-Century Louisiana." *Louisiana Law Review* 76, no. 4 (Summer 2016): 1163-1184.

713. Parise, Agustín. "The Concordancias of Saint-Joseph: A Nineteenth Century Spanish Translation of the Louisiana Civil Code." *Journal of Civil Law Studies* 9, no. 1 (Oct. 2016): 287-328.

714. Park, Sohyeon. "Law and Literature in Late Imperial China and Choson Korea." *Sungkyun Journal of East Asian Studies* 10, no. 2 (Oct. 2010): 229-250.

715. Parker, Kunal M. "Historicising *Blackstone's Commentaries on The Laws of England*: Difference and Sameness in Historical Time." In *Law Books in Action: Essays on the Anglo-American Legal Treatise* (Angela Fernandez & Markus D. Dubber, eds.; Oxford: Hart Publishing, 2012), 22-42.

716. Parma, Rosamond. "The Origin, History, and Compilation of the Casebook." *Law Library Journal* 14, no. 1 (Apr. 1921): 14-19.

717. Parrish, Jenni. "Law Books and Legal Publishing in America, 1760-1840." *Law Library Journal* 72, no. 3 (Summer 1979): 355-452.

718. Paulsen, James W., & James E. Hambleton. "The Official Texas Court Reports: Birth, Death and Resurrection." *Texas Bar Journal* 49, no. 1 (Jan. 1986): 82-83.

719. Paulsen, James W., & James E. Hambleton. "The 'Official' Texas Court Reports: The Rest of the Story." *Texas Bar Journal* 49, no. 8 (Sept. 1986): 842-843.

720. Paulsen, James W., & James E. Hambleton. "A Pocket Part of Posey's: A Daring Expose of Posey's Unreported Cases." *Texas Bar Journal* 53, no. 7 (July 1990): 806-807.

721. Pazzaglini, Peter, & Catharine A. Hawks. *Consilia: A Bibliography of Holdings in the Library of Congress and Certain Other Collections in the United States.* Washington, DC: G.P.O., 1990.

722. Pegues, Frank. "Medieval Origins of Modern Law Reporting." *Cornell Law Quarterly* 38, no. 4 (Summer 1953): 491-510.

723. Pennington, Kenneth. "The Consilia of Baldus De Ubaldis." *Tijdschrift voor Rechtsgeschiedenis / Legal History Review* 56, nos. 1-2 (Jan. 1988): 85-92.

724. Pennington, Kenneth. *Popes, Canonists and Texts, 1150-1550.* Aldershot, UK: Variorum, 1993.

725. Pennington, Kenneth. "Decretal Collections." In *The History of Medieval Canon Law in the Classical Period, 1140-1234: From Gratian to the Decretals of Pope Gregory IX* (Wilfried Hartmann & Kenneth Pennington, eds.; Washington, DC: Catholic University of America Press, 2008), 293-317.

726. Pennington, Kenneth. "The Decretalists 1190 to 1234." In *The History of Medieval Canon Law in the Classical Period, 1140-1234: From Gratian to the Decretals of Gregory IX* (Wilfried Hartmann & Kenneth Pennington, eds.; Washington, DC: Catholic University of America Press, 2008), 211-245.

727. Pennington, Kenneth, & Wolfgang P. Müller. "The Decretists: The Italian School." In *The History of Medieval Canon Law in the Classical Period, 1140-1234: From Gratian to the Decretals of Gregory IX* (Wilfried Hartmann & Kenneth Pennington, eds.; Washington, DC: Catholic University of America Press, 2008), 121-173.

728. Pennington, Kenneth. "The Beginning of Roman Law Jurisprudence and Teaching in the Twelfth Century: The Authenticae." *Rivista Internazionale di Diritto Comune* 22 (2011): 35-53.

729. Pennington, Kenneth. "Western Legal Collections in the Twelfth and Thirteenth Centuries." In *Religious Minorities in Christian, Jewish and Muslim Law (5th-15th Centuries)* (Nora Berend *et al.*, eds.; Turnhout, Belgium: Brepols, 2017), 77-98.

730. Perry, Lisa A. "Legal Handbooks as Rhetoric Books for Common Lawyers in Early Modern England." In *Learning the Law: Teaching and the Transmission of Law in England, 1150-1900* (Jonathan Bush & Alain A. Wijffels, eds.; London: Hambledon Press, 1999), 273-285.

731. Philbin, Patrick F. "The Excepciones Contra Brevia: A Late Thirteenth-Century Teaching Tool." In *Learning the Law: Teaching and the Transmission of Law in England, 1150-1900* (Jonathan Bush & Alain A. Wijffels, eds.; London: Hambledon Press, 1999), 133-156.

732. Phillips, Jim. "A Low Law Counter Treatise? 'Absentees' to 'Wreck' in British North America's First Justice of the Peace Manual." In *Law Books in Action: Essays on the Anglo-American Legal Treatise* (Angela Fernandez & Markus D. Dubber, eds.; Oxford: Hart Publishing, 2012), 202-219.

733. Pihlajamäki, Heikki. "Legal Authorities in the Seventeenth-Century Swedish Empire." In *Authorities in Early Modern Law Courts* (Guido Rossi, ed.; Edinburgh: Edinburgh University Press, 2021), 168-183.

734. Plucknett, Theodore F. T. "Bibliography and Legal History." *Papers of the Bibliographical Society of America* 26, nos. 1/2 (Jan. 1932): 128-142.

735. Plucknett, Theodore F. T. "The Genesis of Coke's Reports." *Cornell Law Quarterly* 27, no. 2 (Feb. 1942): 190-213.

736. Plucknett, Theodore F. T. *Early English Legal Literature.* Cambridge: The University Press, 1958.

737. Poole, Eric. "A Historic Conveyancing Book." In *Collecting and Managing Rare Law Books: Papers Presented at a Conference Celebrating the Dedication of the New Tarlton Law Library, the University of Texas at Austin School of Law, January 7 & 8, 1981* (Roy M. Mersky & Stanley Ferguson, eds.; Dobbs Ferry, NY: Oceana Publications, 1981), 537-546.

738. Poole, Eric. "Old Deeds, and Old Lawbooks." In *Collecting and Managing Rare Law Books: Papers Presented at a Conference Celebrating the Dedication of the New Tarlton Law Library, the University of Texas at Austin School of Law, January 7 & 8, 1981* (Roy M. Mersky & Stanley Ferguson, eds.; Dobbs Ferry, NY: Oceana Publications, 1981), 145-152.

739. Poole, Eric. "West's Symboleography: An Elizabethan Formulary." In *Law and Social Change in British History: Papers Presented to the Bristol Legal History Conference, 14-17 July 1981* (J. A. Guy & H. G. Beale, eds.; London: Royal Historical Society, 1984), 96-106.

740. Powell, Damian. "Coke in Context: Early Modern Legal Observation and Sir Edward Coke's *Reports.*" *Journal of Legal History* 21, no. 3 (Dec. 2000): 33-53.

741. *Pre-Statehood Legal Materials: A Fifty-state Research Guide, Including the District of Columbia and New York City*. Michael Chiorazzi & Marguerite Most, eds. 2 vols. Binghamton, NY: Haworth Press, 2006.

742. Prest, Wilfrid. "The Dialectical Origins of Finch's Law." *Cambridge Law Journal* 36, no. 2 (Nov. 1977): 326-352.

743. Prest, Wilfrid. "Law Books." In *The Cambridge History of the Book in Britain, Volume V, 1695-1830* (Michael Suarez & Michael Turner, eds.; Cambridge: Cambridge University Press, 1998), 791-806.

744. Prest, Wilfrid. "Lay Legal Knowledge in Early Modern England." In *Learning the Law: Teaching and the Transmission of Law in England, 1150-1900* (Jonathan

Bush & Alain A. Wijffels, eds.; London: Hambledon Press, 1999), 303-313.

745. Prest, Wilfrid. "Antipodean Blackstone: The Commentaries Down Under." *Flinders Journal of Law Reform* 6, no. 2 (June 2003): 151-168.

746. Prest, Wilfrid. "Blackstone and Bibliography: In Memoriam Morris Cohen." *Law Library Journal* 104, no. 1 (Winter 2012): 99-113.

747. Prest, Wilfrid. "Antipodean Blackstone." In *Reinterpreting Blackstone's Commentaries: A Seminal Text in National and International Contexts* (Wilfrid Prest, ed.; Oxford, UK: Hart Publishing, 2014), 145-165.

748. Prest, Wilfrid, & Michael Widener. *250 Years of Blackstone's Commentaries: An Exhibition.* Buffalo, N.Y.: William S. Hein & Co., 2015.

749. Pritchett, Carla Downer. "Case Law Reporters in Nineteenth-Century Louisiana." In *A Law Unto Itself?: Essays in the New Louisiana Legal History* (Warren M. Billings & Mark F. Fernandez, eds.; Baton Rouge: Louisiana State University Press, 2001), 58-76.

750. Pruitt, Paul M., Jr. "A Frontier Justinian: An Introduction to the Life and Writings of Harry Toulmin, Territorial Judge of Mississippi and Alabama." *Unbound: An Annual Review of Legal History and Rare Books* 2 (2009): 45-67. https://www.aallnet.org/lhrbsis/resources-publications/unbound/

751. Pruitt, Paul M., Jr., David I. Durham, & Michael H. Hoeflich. *Law and Miscellaneous Works: The Lives and Careers of Joel White and Amand Pfister, Booksellers and Publishers.* Tuscaloosa, AL: University of Alabama School of Law, 2019.

752. Pryce, Huw. "The Prologues to the Welsh Lawbooks." *Bulletin of the Board of Celtic Studies* 33 (1986), 151-187.

166

753. Pryce, Huw. "Lawbooks and Literacy in Medieval Wales." *Speculum* 75, no. 1 (Jan. 2000), 29-67.

754. Pryce, Huw. "The Context and Purpose of the Earliest Welsh Lawbooks." *Cambrian Medieval Celtic Studies* 39 (Summer 2000): 39-63.

755. Pugsley, David. *Justinian's Digest and the Compilers.* 2 vols. Exeter, UK: Faculty of Law, University of Exeter, 1995.

756. Pugsley, David. "More Simple Questions about Justinian's Digest." *Fundamina: A Journal of Legal History* 16, no. 1 (Jan. 2010): 335-345.

757. Putnam, Bertha Haven. *Early Treatises on the Practice of the Justices of the Peace in the Fifteenth and Sixteenth Centuries.* Oxford: Clarendon Press, 1924.

758. Qiu, Fangzhe. "Law, Law-Books and Tradition in Early Medieval Ireland." In *Law | Book | Culture in the Middle Ages* (Thom Gobbitt, ed.; Leiden: Koninklijke Brill NV, 2021), 126-146.

759. Rabalais, Raphael J. "The Influence of Spanish Laws and Treatises on the Jurisprudence of Louisiana: 1762-1828." *Louisiana Law Review* 42, no. 5 (1982): 1485-1508.

760. Rabban, David M. "Hammond's Blackstone and the Historical School of American Jurisprudence." In *Blackstone and His Critics* (Anthony Page & Wilfrid Prest, eds.; Oxford: Hart Publishing, 2018), 173-191.

761. Rabbie, Edwin. "The History and Reconstruction of Hugo Grotius' Library: A Survey of the Results of Former Studies with an Indication of New Lines of Approach." In *Bibliothecae Selectae da Cusano a Leopardi* (Eugenio Canone, ed.; Florence: Olschki, 1993), 119-137.

762. Radding, Charles M., & Antonio Ciaralli. "The Corpus Iuris Civilis in the Middle Ages: A Case Study in Historiography and Medieval History." *Zeitschrift der*

Savigny-Stiftung für Rechtsgeschichte: Romanistiche Abteilung 117, no. 1 (2000): 274-310.

763. Radding, Charles M., & Antonio Ciaralli. *The* Corpus Iuris Civilis *in the Middle Ages: Manuscripts and Transmission from the Sixth Century to the Juristic Revival.* Leiden; Boston: Brill, 2007.

764. Radding, Charles M. "Reviving Justinian's Corpus: The Case of the Code." In *Law Before Gratian: Law in Western Europe c. 500-1100* (Per Andersen *et al.*, eds.; Copenhagen: DJØF Publishing, 2007), 35-50.

765. Radding, Charles M. "Law Books." In *The European Book in the Twelfth Century* (Erik Kwakkel, ed.; Cambridge: Cambridge University Press, 2018), 293-310.

766. Rahmatian, Andreas. "The Role of Institutional Writers in Scots Law." *Juridical Review* 2018, no. 1: 42-63.

767. Raisch, Marylin J. "Codes and Hypertext: The Intertextuality of International and Comparative Law." *Syracuse Journal of International Law & Commerce* 35, no. 2 (Spring 2008): 309-339.

768. Ramsay, Nigel. "Law." In *The Cambridge History of the Book in Britain, Volume II, 1100-1400* (Cambridge: Cambridge University Press, 2008), 250-290.

769. Reed, Arthur W. "The Editor of Sir Thomas More's English Works: William Rastell." *The Library: Transactions of the Bibliographical Society*, 4th Series 4, no. 1 (June 1923): 25-49.

770. Reeves, Jesse S. "The First Edition of Grotius's *De Jure Belli ac Pacis*, 1625." *American Journal of International Law* 19, no. 1 (Jan. 1925): 12-22.

771. Reeves, Jesse S. "Grotius, *De Jure Belli ac Pacis*: A Bibliographic Account." *American Journal of International Law* 19, no. 2 (Apr. 1925): 251-262.

772. Reich, Peter L. "Siete Partidas in My Saddlebags: The Transmission of Hispanic Law from Antebellum

168

Louisiana to Texas and California." *Tulane European & Civil Law Forum* 22 (2007): 79-88.

773. Reid, Kenneth G. C. "From Text-Book to Book of Authority: The *Principles* of George Joseph Bell." *Edinburgh Law Review* 15, no. 1 (Jan. 2011): 6-32.

774. Reiter, Eric H. "Imported Books, Imported Ideas: Reading European Jurisprudence in Mid-Nineteenth Century Quebec." *Law and History Review* 22, no. 3 (Fall 2004): 445-492.

775. Reynolds, Sue. "Redmond Barry and the Foundation of the Library of the Supreme Court of Victoria: Legal Legacies." *Australian Journal of Legal History* 13, no. 2 (2009): 259-268.

776. Reynolds, Thomas H. "Medieval Canon and Roman Law: An Introductory Bibliographical Essay." In *Collecting and Managing Rare Law Books: Papers Presented at a Conference Celebrating the Dedication of the New Tarlton Law Library, the University of Texas at Austin School of Law, January 7 & 8, 1981* (Roy M. Mersky & Stanley Ferguson, eds.; Dobbs Ferry, NY: Oceana Publications, 1981), 317-356.

777. Rhodes, Dennis E. "Italian City and Regional Statutes, 1473-1600, in the British Library." *British Library Journal* 3, no. 11 (Spring 1977): 56-58.

778. Rial Costas, Benito. "Marketing a New Legal Code in Fifteenth Century Castile: A Case Study of the Interactions between Crown, Law and Printing." In *Books in Motion in Early Modern Europe: Beyond Production, Circulation and Consumption* (Daniel Bellingradt, Paul Nelles & Jeroen Salman, eds.; London: Palgrave Macmillan, 2017), 87-108.

779. Ribeiro da Silva, Airton, Jr. "Magistrates' Travelling Libraries: The Circulation of Normative Knowledge in the Portuguese Empire of the Late 18th Century." *Rechtsgeschichte - Legal History (Rg)* 29 (2021): 128-141.

780. Richardson, H. G., & George Sayles. "The Early Statutes." *Law Quarterly Review* 50, no. 2 (Apr. 1934): 201-223; *Law Quarterly Review* 50, no. 4 (Oct. 1934): 540-571.

781. Richardson, H. G. *Bracton, the Problem of his Text.* London: Selden Society, 1965.

782. Riisøy, Anne Irene. "From Law to List." *Bulletin of Medieval Canon Law* 26 (2004-2006): 153-168.

783. Ritz, Wilfred J. "The Francis Hopkinson Law Reports: The Originals and the Reprints." *Law Library Journal* 74, no. 2 (Spring 1981): 298-323.

784. Ritz, Wilfred J., comp. *American Judicial Proceedings First Printed Before 1801: An Analytical Bibliography.* Westport, CT: Greenwood, 1984.

785. Rivers, Kimberly A. "Learning and Remembering Canon Law in the Fifteenth Century: The *Ars et doctrina studendi et docendi* of Juan Alfonso de Benavente." In *From Learning to Love: Schools, Law, and Pastoral Care in the Middle Ages: Essays in Honour of Joseph W. Goering* (Tristan Sharp, ed.; Toronto: Pontifical Institute of Mediaeval Studies 2017), 266-290.

786. Roark, Lillian. *Translation of Biographies of Noted Spanish Commentators.* San Francisco [publisher not identified], 1929?.

787. Roberts, Alfred Adrian. *A South African Legal Bibliography: Being a Bio-bibliographical Survey and Law-finder of the Roman and Roman-Dutch Legal Literature in Southern Africa with an Historical Chart, Notes on All the Judges since 1828, and Other Appendices.* Pretoria: [The author], 1942.

788. Robinson, Robert B. "The Two *Institutes* of Thomas Wood: A Study in Eighteenth Century Legal Scholarship." *American Journal of Legal History* 35, no. 4 (Oct. 1991): 432-458.

789. Rocher, Ludo. "Law Books in an Oral Culture: The Indian Dharmasastras." *Proceedings of the American Philosophical Society* 137, no. 2 (June 1993): 254-267.

790. Rodgers, Christopher P. "Continental Literature and the Development of the Common Law by the King's Bench: c. 1750-1800." In *The Courts and the Development of Commercial Law* (Vito Piergiovanni, ed.; Berlin: Duncker & Humblot, 1987), 161-194.

791. Roeber, A. G. "'The Scrutiny of the Ill Natured Ignorant Vulgar': Lawyers and Print Culture in Virginia, 1716 to 1774." *The Virginia Magazine of History and Biography* 91, no. 4 (Oct. 1983): 387-417.

792. Roebuck, Derek. "Sources for the History of Arbitration: A Bibliographical Introduction." *Arbitration International* 14, no. 3 (Sept. 1998): 237-343.

793. Rogers, Ralph V. "The Editing and Publication of the Year Books of the Reign of Edward III." *Law Library Journal* 44, no. 2 (May 1951) 71-78.

794. Rohrbach, Lena. "Repositioning Jónsbók: Rearrangements of the Law in Fourteenth- Century Iceland." In *Legislation and State Formation: Norway and Its Neighbours in the Middle Ages* (Steinar Imsen, ed.; Trondheim: Tapir, 2013), 183-209.

795. Rohrbach, Lena. "Matrix of the Law? A Material Study of the Text of Konungsbók." In *The Power of the Book: Medial Approaches to Medieval Nordic Legal Manuscripts* (Lena Rohrbach, ed.; Berlin: Nordeuropa-Institut der Humboldt-Universität, 2014), 99-128.

796. Roskell, J. S. "A Consideration of Certain Aspects and Problems of the English 'Modus Tenendi Parliamentum'." *Bulletin of the John Rylands Library* 50, no. 2 (Mar. 1968): 411-442.

797. Ross, Richard J. "The Commoning of the Common Law: The Renaissance Debate over Printing English Law,

1520-1640." *University of Pennsylvania Law Review* 146, no. 2 (1998): 323-461.

798. Ross, Richard J. "The Memorial Culture of Early Modern English Lawyers: Memory as Keyword, Shelter, and Identity, 1560-1640." *Yale Journal of Law & the Humanities* 10, no. 2 (Summer 1998): 229-326.

799. Roughen, Patrick F., Jr. "Francis Lieber and the South Carolina College Library: An Examination of a Scholar's Academic Library Use." *Australian & New Zealand Law & History E-Journal*, Refereed Paper No. 3 (2013). http://www.austlii.edu.au/au/journals/ANZLawHisteJl/2013/4.html

800. Rowan, Steven W. "The German Works of Ulrich Zasius." *Manuscripta* 21, no. 3 (Nov. 1977): 131-143.

801. Rowan, Steven W. "Jurists and the Printing Press in Germany: The First Century." In *Print and Culture in the Renaissance: Essays on the Advent of Printing in Europe* (Gerald P. Tyson & Sylvia S. Wagonheim, eds.; Newark: University of Delaware Press, 1986), 74-89.

802. Rowan, Steven W. *Ulrich Zasius: A Jurist in the German Renaissance, 1461-1535.* Frankfurt am Main: V. Klostermann, 1987.

803. Rudolph, Julia. "That 'Blunderbuss of Law': Giles Jacob, Abridgment, and Print Culture." *Studies in Eighteenth-Century Culture* 37 (2008): 197-215.

804. Rudolph, Julia. "Law Books, Legal Knowledge, and Enlightened Encyclopedism." Chapter 2 in Julia Rudolph, *Common Law and Enlightenment in England, 1689-1750* (Woodbridge: Boydell & Brewer, 2013), 30-82.

805. Rueda Ramírez, Pedro. "Law Books in the Hispanic Atlantic World: Spaces, Agents and the Consumption of Texts in the Early Modern Period." *Rechtsgeschichte - Legal History (Rg)* 29 (2021): 100-113.

172

806. Sass, Stephen L. "Research in Roman Law: A Guide to the Sources and Their English Translations." *Law Library Journal* 56, no. 3 (Aug. 1963): 210-233.

807. Sass, Stephen L. "Medieval Roman Law: A Guide to the Sources and Literature." *Law Library Journal* 58, no. 2 (May 1965): 130-159.

808. Satterley, Renae. "The Libraries of the Inns of Court: An Examination of Their Historical Influence." *Library History* 24, no. 3 (Sept. 2008): 208-219.

809. Saunders, Myra K. "California Legal History: A Review of Spanish and Mexican Legal Institutions." *Law Library Journal* 87, no. 3 (Summer 1995): 487-514.

810. Savelli, Rodolfo. "The Censoring of Law Books." In *Church, Censorship and Culture in Early Modern Italy* (Gigliola Fragnito, ed.; Cambridge, UK: Cambridge University Press, 2001), 223-253.

811. Sawyer, William H. "Historical and Bibliographical Notes on the Sheets of New Hampshire Statutes." *Law Library Journal* 41, no. 1 (Feb. 1948): 1-10.

812. Schauer, Frederick, & Virginia J. Wise. "Bundling, Boundary Setting, and the Privatization of Legal Information." In *Market-Based Governance* (John D. Donahue & Joseph S. Nye, eds.; Washington, D.C.: Brookings Institution Press, 2002), 128-142.

813. Schneider, Herbert. "The Sung Constitutions of 1792: An Essay on Propaganda in the Revolutionary Song." In *Music and the French Revolution* (Malcolm Boyd, ed.; Cambridge, UK: Cambridge University Press, 1992), 236-275.

814. Schoeck, R. J. "The Libraries of Common Lawyers in the Renaissance." *Manuscripta* 6, no. 3 (Oct. 1962): 155-167.

815. Scholz, Luca. "Visualizing Generational Change in Early Modern Law Dissertations." *Current Research in Digital History* 5 (2022). https://doi.org/10.31835/crdh.2022.01

816. Scholz, Luca. "A Distant Reading of Legal Dissertations from German Universities in the Seventeenth Century." *The Historical Journal* 65, no. 2 (Mar. 2022), 297-327.

817. Schrage, Eltjo J. H. "Descendit Ad Inferos: And Belial Sued Jesus Christ for Trespass." In *Critical Studies in Ancient Law, Comparative Law and Legal History* (John W. Cairns & Olivia F. Robinson, eds.; Oxford: Hart Publishing, 2001), 353-363.

818. Schulz, Fritz. "A New Approach to Bracton." *Seminar (Jurist)* 2 (1944): 41-50.

819. Schulze, W. G. "A Conspectus of South African Legal Periodicals: Past to Present." *Fundamina: A Journal of Legal History* 19, no. 1 (Jan. 2013): 61-105.

820. Schwartz, Bernard. "Ten Greatest Law Books." In Bernard Schwartz, *A Book of Legal Lists: The Best and Worst in American Law with 100 Court and Judge Trivia Questions* (New York: Oxford University Press, 1997), 189-209.

821. Seer, Gitelle, & Jill Sidford. "The Evolution of Law Firm Libraries: A Preliminary History." In *Law Librarianship: Historical Perspectives* (Laura N. Gasaway & Michael G. Chiorazzi, eds.; Littleton, CO: F. B. Rothman, 1996), 77-109.

822. Seipp, David J. "The Mirror of Justices." In *Learning the Law: Teaching and the Transmission of Law in England, 1150-1900* (Jonathan Bush & Alain A. Wijffels, eds.; London: Hambledon Press, 1999), 85-112.

823. Seipp, David J. "The Law's Many Bodies, and the Manuscript Tradition in English Legal History." *Journal of Legal History* 25, no. 1 (Apr. 2004): 74-83.

824. Seipp, David J. "Year Book Men." In *English Legal History and Its Sources: Essays in Honour of Sir John Baker*, (David Ibbetson *et al.*, eds.; Cambridge, UK: Cambridge University Press, 2019), 3-22.

174

825. Sellers, Nicholas. "The Smith Nicholas Law Library." *Law Library Journal* 83, no. 3 (Summer 1991): 463-478.

826. Sellers, Nicholas. "The Fielding Lewis Turner Law Library." *Law Library Journal* 86, no. 3 (Summer 1994): 597-604.

827. Senior, W. "Early Writers on Maritime Law." *Law Quarterly Review* 37, no. 3 (1921): 323-336.

828. Senior, W. "Roman Law MSS. in England." *Law Quarterly Review* 47, no. 3 (July 1931): 337-344.

829. Senzel, Howard T. "Looseleafing the Flow: An Anecdotal History of One Technology for Updating." *American Journal of Legal History* 44, no. 2 (Apr. 2000): 115-197.

830. Shapiro, Barbara J. *Law Reform in Early Modern England: Crown, Parliament and the Press.* Oxford: Hart, 2019.

831. Shapiro, Fred R. "Origins of Bibliometrics, Citation Indexing, and Citation Analysis: The Neglected Legal Literature." *Journal of the American Society for Information Science* 43, no.5 (1992): 337-339. Reprinted: Fred R. Shapiro, *Collected Papers on Legal Citation Analysis* (Littleton, CO: Fred B. Rothman Publications, 2001), 155-158.

832. Shapiro, Fred R. "The Most-Cited Law Review Articles Revisited." *Chicago-Kent Law Review* 71, no. 3 (1996): 751-780. Reprinted: Fred R. Shapiro, *Collected Papers on Legal Citation Analysis* (Littleton, CO: Fred B. Rothman Publications, 2001), 85-114.

833. Shapiro, Fred R., & Michelle Pearse. "The Most-Cited Law Review Articles of All Time." *Michigan Law Review* 110, no. 8 (June 2012): 1483-1520.

834. Shapiro, Fred R., & Julie Graves Krishnaswami. "The Secret History of the Bluebook." *Minnesota Law Review* 100, no. 4 (Apr. 2016): 1563-1598.

835. Shapiro, Fred R. "The Most-Cited Legal Scholars Revisited." *University of Chicago Law Review* 88, no. 7 (Nov. 2021): 1595-1618.

836. Shea, Dorothy. "Legal Publishing in Tasmania." *Australian Law Librarian* 5, no. 4 (Dec. 1997): 250-257.

837. Shepard, E. Lee. "The First Law Journals in Virginia." *Law Library Journal* 79, no. 1 (Winter 1987): 33-52.

838. Sheppard, Stephen M. "Casebooks, Commentaries, and Curmudgeons: An Introductory History of Law in the Lecture Hall." *Iowa Law Review* 82, no. 2 (Jan. 1997): 547-644.

839. Sheppard, Stephen M. "Legal Jambalaya." In *Re-interpreting Blackstone's Commentaries: A Seminal Text in National and International Contexts* (Wilfrid Prest, ed.; Oxford, UK: Hart Publishing, 2014), 95-104.

840. Simpson, A. W. B. "Keilwey's Reports, temp. Henry VII and Henry VIII." *Law Quarterly Review* 73 (Jan. 1957): 89-105.

841. Simpson, A. W. B. "The Circulation of Yearbooks in the Late Fifteenth Century." *Law Quarterly Review* 73 (Oct. 1957): 492-505.

842. Simpson, A. W. B. "The Source and Function of the Later Year Books." *Law Quarterly Review* 87 (Jan. 1971): 94-118.

843. Simpson, A. W. B. "The Rise and Fall of the Legal Treatise: Legal Principles and the Forms of Legal Literature." *University of Chicago Law Review* 48, no. 3 (Summer 1981): 632-679.

844. Simpson, A. W. B. "The Legal Treatise and Legal Theory." In *Law, Litigants and the Legal Profession* (E. W. Ives & A. H. Manchester, eds.; London: Royal Historical Society, 1983), 11-29.

845. Sirks, Adriaan Johan Boudewijn. *The Theodosian Code: A Study*. Friedrichsdorf: Éditions Tortuga, 2007.

846. Sirks, Adriaan Johan Boudewijn. "Bijnkershoek as Author and Elegant Jurist." *Tijdschrift voor Rechtsgeschiedenis / Legal History Review* 79, no. 2 (Jan. 2011): 229-252.

847. Skemer, Don C. "Reading the Law: Statute Books and the Private Transmission of Legal Knowledge in Late Medieval England." In *Learning the Law: Teaching and the Transmission of Law in England, 1150-1900* (Jonathan Bush & Alain A. Wijffels, eds.; London: Hambledon Press, 1999), 113-131.

848. Sleeman, Bill. "Tracing the Origin of the Elbridge T. Gerry Collection at the Supreme Court of the United States Library." *Law Library Lights* 62, no. 3 (Spring 2019): 1-5.

849. Smidt, J. Th. de. *Old Law Books from the Libraries of the 'Raad van Justitie' (High Court) and J.N. van Dessin (South African Library).* Leiden: Grafaria, 1998.

850. Smidt, J. Th. de. "An Elderly, Noble Lady: The Old Books Collection in the Library of the Supreme Court of the Netherlands." In *The Old Library of the Supreme Court of the Netherlands* (J. G. B. Pikkemaat, ed.; Hilversum: Verloren, 2008), 39-68.

851. Smith, Patterson. "Thomas McDade and the Annals of Murder." *AB Bookman's Weekly* 97, no. 17 (Apr. 22, 1996): 1613-1623.

852. Smith, Robert S. "The *Llibre del Consolat de Mar*: A Bibliography." *Law Library Journal* 33, no. 6 (Nov. 1940): 387-396.

853. Sobecki, Sebastian. "Certain Obscure and Dark Terms: John Rastell and the First English Law Lexicon, 1524." In *Dynamic Translations in the European Renaissance* (Philiep Bossier *et al.*, eds.; Manziana: Vecchiarelli, 2011), 73-84.

854. Sobecki, Sebastian. *Unwritten Verities: The Making of England's Vernacular Legal Culture, 1463-1549.* Notre Dame, IN: University of Notre Dame Press, 2015.

855. Soetermeer, Frank. "Between Codicology and Legal History: Pecia Manuscripts of Legal Texts." *Manuscripta* 49, no. 2 (2005): 247-267.

856. Solon Cristobal, Kasia. "From Law in Blackletter to Blackletter Law." *Law Library Journal* 108, no. 2 (Spring 2016): 181-216.

857. Somos, Mark. "The Unseen History of International Law: A Census Bibliography of Hugo Grotius's *De iure belli ac pacis*." *Grotiana* 40, no. 1 (Dec. 2019): 173-179.

858. Sparrow, John. "The Earlier Owners of Books in John Selden's Library." *Bodleian Quarterly Record* 6 (1931): 263-271.

859. Spiller, Peter. "The Development of Law Reporting in New Zealand." *New Zealand Law Journal* 1994 (Feb. 1994): 75-80.

860. *Stair Tercentenary Studies*. David M. Walker, ed. Edinburgh: The Stair Society, 1981.

861. Stauffer, Jill. "'You people talk from paper': Indigenous Law, Western Legalism, and the Cultural Variability of Law's Materials." *Law Text Culture* 23 (2019), 40-57. https://ro.uow.edu.au/ltc/vol23/iss1/4

862. Stebbings, Chantal. "Law Reporting and Law-Making: The Missing Link in Nineteenth-Century Tax Law." In *Networks and Connections in Legal History* (Michael Lobban & Ian Williams, eds.; Cambridge, UK: Cambridge University Press, 2020), 285-306.

863. Stebbins, Howard L. "Outline of Massachusetts Statute Law Publications." *Law Library Journal* 20, no. 3 (Oct. 1927): 72-84.

864. Stein, Peter. "The Source of the Romano-Canonical Part of Regiam Maiestatem." *Scottish Historical Review* 48, no. 146 (Oct. 1969): 107-123.

865. Stein, Peter. "The Development of the Institutional System." In *Studies in Justinian's Institutes in Memory*

of J. A. C. Thomas (Peter G. Stein & A. D. E. Lewis, eds.; London: Sweet & Maxwell, 1983), 151-163.

866. Stein, Peter. "England and Continental Legal Literature." In *Englische und kontinentale Rechtsgeschichte: ein Forschungsprojekt* (Helmut Coing & Knut Wolfgang Nörr, eds.; Berlin: Duncker & Humblot, 1985), 77-81.

867. Stein, Peter. "Civil Law Reports and the Case of San Marino." In Peter Stein, *The Character and Influence of the Roman Civil Law: Historical Essays* (London: Hambledon Press, 1988), 115-130.

868. Stein, Peter. "Thomas Legge: A Sixteenth Century English Civilian and His Books." In Peter Stein, *The Character and Influence of the Roman Civil Law: Historical Essays* (London: Hambledon Press, 1988), 197-208.

869. Stein, Peter. "Justinian's Compilation: Classical Legacy and Legal Source." *Tulane European & Civil Law Forum* 8 (1993): 1-16.

870. Stein, Peter. "The Ius Commune and its Demise." *Journal of Legal History* 25, no. 2 (Aug. 2004): 161-168.

871. Steiner, Mark E. "General Catalogue of Law Books, Alphabetically Classified by Subject (1859)." *Legal Reference Services Quarterly* 18, no. 1 (1999): 47-121.

872. Steiner, Mark E. "Abraham Lincoln and the Rule of Law Books." *Marquette Law Review* 93, no. 4 (Summer 2010): 1283-1324.

873. Stern, Simon. "The Case and the Exceptions: Creating Instrumental Texts in Law and Literature." In *Producing the Eighteenth-Century Book: Writers and Publishers in England* (Pat Rogers & Laura Runge, eds.; Newark: University of Delaware Press, 2009), 95-116.

874. Stern, Simon. "Margins of Authority: Coke's *Institutes* and the Epistemology of the String Cite." *Law and Humanities* 11, no. 1 (Summer 2017): 121-136.

875. Stevens, Kevin M. "Publishing the *Constitutiones Dominii Mediolanensis* (1541-1552): New Revelations." *La Bibliofilia* 116, nos. 1-3 (Jan.-Dec. 2014): 215-229.

876. Stevenson, Noel C. "The Glorious Uncertainty of the Law 1846-1851." *Journal of the State Bar of California* 28, no. 5 (Sept.-Oct. 1953): 374-380.

877. Stolte, Bernard H. "The *Partes* of the Digest in the Codex Florentinus." *Subseciva Groningana: Studies in Roman and Byzantine Law* 1 (1984), 69-91.

878. Stolte, Bernard H. "Some Thoughts on the Early History of the Digest Text." *Subseciva Groningana: Studies in Roman and Byzantine Law* 6 (1999), 103-120.

879. Stolte, Bernard H. "Codification in Byzantium: From Justinian to Leo VI." In *Diverging Paths? The Shapes of Power and Institutions in Medieval Christendom and Islam* (John Hudson & Ana Rodríguez, eds.; Leiden: Brill, 2014), 55-74.

880. Stolte, Bernard H. "Joannes Leunclavius (1541-1594), Civilian or Byzantinist?" In *Reassessing Legal Humanism and Its Claims: Petere Fontes?* (Paul J. du Plessis & John W. Cairns, eds.; Edinburgh: Edinburgh University Press, 2016), 194-210.

881. Stone, Marilyn. "Las Siete Partidas in America: Problems of Cultural Transmission in the Translation of Legal Signs." In *Translation and the Law* (Marshall Morris, ed.; Philadelphia: John Benjamins Publishing, 1995), 281-291.

882. Stotter, Lawrence H. *To Put Asunder: The Laws of Matrimonial Strife; An Introduction to the Seminal Anglo-American Literature and Laws of Domestic Relations Up to the Year 1900, with Supporting Bibliography and Comments.* Berkeley: Regent Press, 2011.

883. Strickland, Rennard. "Corpus of the Written Cherokee Laws." *Law Library Journal* 67, no. 1 (Feb. 1974): 110-119.

884. Stump, Phillip. "The Official Acta of the Council of Constance in the Edition of Mansi." In *The Two Laws: Studies in Medieval History Dedicated to Stephan Kuttner* (Laurent Mayali & Stephanie A.J. Tibbets, eds.; Washington: The Catholic University of America, 1990), 221-239.

885. Surrency, Erwin C., Richard Sloane, & Mary L. Fisher. "Bicentennial History of American Law Publishing." *Law Library Journal* 69, no. 4 (Nov. 1976): 576-593.

886. Surrency, Erwin C. "Law Reports in the United States." *American Journal of Legal History* 25, no. 1 (Jan. 1981): 48-66.

887. Surrency, Erwin C. "English Reports Printed in America." *Legal Reference Services Quarterly* 3, no. 2 (Spring 1983): 9-16.

888. Surrency, Erwin C. "The Beginnings of American Legal Literature." *American Journal of Legal History* 31, no. 3 (July 1987): 207-220.

889. Surrency, Erwin C. "The Publication of Federal Laws: A Short History." *Law Library Journal* 79, no. 3 (Summer 1987): 469-484.

890. Surrency, Erwin C. *A History of American Law Publishing.* New York: Oceana Publications, 1990.

891. Swain, Warren. "The Legal Treatise and the History of the Common Law." *Queensland Legal Yearbook 2014*, 132-150. https://archive.sclqld.org.au/sclpub/queensland-legal-yearbook/2014/queensland-legal-yearbook-2014.pdf

892. Sweet & Maxwell. *A Legal Bibliography of the British Commonwealth of Nations.* 8 vols. London: Sweet & Maxwell, 1955-1964.

893. Sweet & Maxwell. *Sweet & Maxwell's Guide to Law Reports and Statutes.* 4th ed. London: Sweet & Maxwell, 1962.

894. Swygert, Michael L., & Jon W. Bruce. "The Historical Origins, Founding, and Early Development of Student-Edited Law Reviews." *Hastings Law Journal* 36, no. 5 (May 1985): 739-792.

895. Tanzini, Lorenzo. "The *Consulate of the Sea* and its Fortunes in Late Medieval Mediterranean Countries." In *Courts of Chivalry and Admiralty in Late Medieval Europe* (Anthony Musson & Nigel Ramsay, eds.; Woodbridge: Boydell Press, 2018), 171-185.

896. Tarter, Brent. "The Library of the Council of Colonial Virginia." In *"Esteemed bookes of lawe" and the Legal Culture of Early Virginia* (Warren M. Billings & Brent Tarter, eds.; Charlottesville: University of Virginia Press, 2017), 37-56.

897. Taussig, Anthony. "William Rastell and the Development of the Law Book for Students and Practitioners." In *Language and the Law: Proceedings of a Conference, December 6-8, 2001, Tarlton Law Library, The University of Texas at Austin* (Marlyn Robinson, ed.; Buffalo, N.Y.: William S. Hein & Co., 2003), 31-44.

898. Taussig, Anthony. "A Revolution in Legal Publishing: The Earliest Booksellers' Catalogues of English Law Books." Parts 1-2. *The Book Collector* 71, no. 1 (Spring 2022): 57-72; 71, no. 2 (Summer 2022): 288-300.

899. Taylor, Alice. "What Does *Regiam maiestatem* Actually Say (and What Does it Mean)?" In *Common Law, Civil Law, and Colonial Law: Essays in Comparative Legal History from the Twelfth to the Twentieth Centuries* (William Eves, *et al.*, eds; Cambridge, UK: Cambridge University Press, 2021), 47-85.

900. Taylor, Betty W. "American Law Library Book Catalogs." *Law Library Journal* 69, no. 3 (Aug. 1976): 347-356.

901. Taylor, Betty W. "American Legal Bibliography 1860-1900." In *Collecting and Managing Rare Law Books: Papers Presented at a Conference Celebrating the Dedi-*

182

cation of the New Tarlton Law Library, the University of Texas at Austin School of Law, January 7 & 8, 1981 (Roy M. Mersky & Stanley Ferguson, eds.; Dobbs Ferry, NY: Oceana Publications, 1981), 133-143.

902. Taylor, Betty W., & Robert J. Munro. *American Law Publishing, 1860-1900.* 4 vols. Dobbs Ferry, NY: Glanville Publications, 1984.

903. Tesar, Linda K. "Forensic Bibliography: Reconstructing the Library of George Wythe." *Law Library Journal* 105, no. 1 (Winter 2013): 57-77.

904. Tesar, Linda K. "The Library Reveals the Man: George Wythe, Legal and Classical Scholar." In *"Esteemed bookes of lawe" and the Legal Culture of Early Virginia* (Warren M. Billings & Brent Tarter, eds.; Charlottesville: University of Virginia Press, 2017), 113-136.

905. Thorne, Samuel E. "St. Germain's Doctor and Student." *The Library: Transactions of the Bibliographical Society*, 4th series 10, no. 4 (Mar. 1930): 421-426.

906. Thorne, Samuel E. "Fitzherbert's Abridgement." *Law Library Journal* 29, no. 3 (July 1936): 59-62.

907. Thorne, Samuel E. "Gilbert de Thornton's Summa de Legibus." *University of Toronto Law Journal* 7, no. 1 (Lent Term 1947): 1-26.

908. Toomer, G. J. "Selden's 'Historie of Tithes': Genesis, Publication, Aftermath." *Huntington Library Quarterly* 65, nos. 3/4 (2002): 345-378.

909. Toomer, G. J. *John Selden: A Life in Scholarship.* 2 vols. Oxford, UK: Oxford University Press, 2009.

910. Topulos, Katherine. "A Common Lawyer's Bookshelf Recreated: An Annotated Bibliography of a Collection of Sixteenth-Century English Law Books." *Law Library Journal* 84, no. 4 (Fall 1992): 641-686.

911. Trelles, Oscar M. II. "Spanish Law and Its Influence in the Americas." In *Collecting and Managing Rare Law Books: Papers Presented at a Conference Celebrating*

the Dedication of the New Tarlton Law Library, the University of Texas at Austin School of Law, January 7 & 8, 1981 (Roy M. Mersky & Stanley Ferguson, eds.; Dobbs Ferry, NY: Oceana Publications, 1981), 165-292.

912. Tucker, E. F. J. *"The Mirror of Justices*: Its Authorship and Preoccupations." *Irish Jurist* 9, no. 1 (Summer 1974): 99-109.

913. Tucker, John H., Jr. "Source Books of Louisiana Law." Parts I-III. *Tulane Law Review* 6, no. 2 (Feb. 1932): 280-300; 7, no. 1 (Dec. 1932): 82-95; 8, no. 3 (Apr. 1934): 396-405.

914. Tullis, Sarah. "Glanvill after Glanvill: The Afterlife of a Medieval Legal Treatise." In *Laws, Lawyers and Texts: Studies in Medieval Legal History in Honour of Paul Brand* (Suzanne Jenks *et al.*, eds.; Leiden: Brill, 2012), 327-359.

915. Van Ittersum, Martine Julia. "Preparing *Mare liberum* for the Press: Hugo Grotius' Rewriting of Chapter 12 of *De iure praedae* in November-December 1608." *Grotiana* 26-28, no. 1 (Jan. 2007): 246-280.

916. Van Ittersum, Martine Julia. "Confiscated Manuscripts and Books: What Happened to the Personal Library and Archive of Hugo Grotius Following His Arrest on Charges of High Treason in August 1618?" In *Lost Books: Reconstructing the Print World of Pre-Industrial Europe* (Flavia Bruni & Andrew Pettegree, eds.; Leiden: Brill, 2016), 362-385.

917. Van Ittersum, Martine Julia. "The Working Methods of Hugo Grotius: Which Sources Did He Use and How Did He Use Them in His Early Writings on Natural Law Theory?" In *Reassessing Legal Humanism and Its Claims: Petere Fontes?* (Paul J. du Plessis & John W. Cairns, eds.; Edinburgh: Edinburgh University Press, 2016), 154-193.

918. Van Niekerk, J. P. "An Introduction to South African Law Reports and Reporters, 1828 to 1910." *Fundamina:*

A Journal of Legal History 19, no. 1 (Jan. 2013): 106-145.

919. Van Niekerk, J. P., & Gardiol van Niekerk. "A Tale of Two Translations: Van Leeuwen and Van der Linden and the Application of Roman-Dutch Law at the Cape in the 1820s; to Which is Appended a Transcription of PB Borcherds' 1822 Translation of Book II of Van der Linden's *Koopmans Handboek.*" *Fundamina: A Journal of Legal History* 24, no. 2 (Nov. 2018): 174-257.

920. Van Nifterik, Gustaaf. "Observations on the Legal Observations." *Grotiana* 40, no. 1 (Dec. 2019): 1-6.

921. Van Warmelo, Paul. "The Institutes of Justinian as Students' Manual." In *Studies in Justinian's Institutes in Memory of J. A. C. Thomas* (Peter G. Stein & A. D. E. Lewis, eds.; London: Sweet & Maxwell, 1983), 164-180.

922. Vance, John Thomas. *The Background of Hispanic-American Law: Legal Sources and Juridical Literature of Spain.* New York: Central Book Co., 1943. Reprinted: Westport, CT: Hyperion Press, 1979.

923. Vinci, Stefano. "Liber Belial: A Vademecum for Roman-Canonical Procedure in Europe." *Forum Historiae Iuris* (2015). https://forhistiur.net/2015-01-vinci/.

924. *Virginia Law Books: Essays and Bibliographies.* William Hamilton Bryson, ed. Philadelphia: American Philosophical Society, 2000.

925. Vogenauer, Stefan. "Law Journals in Nineteenth-Century England." *Edinburgh Law Review* 12, no. 1 (Jan. 2008): 26-50.

926. von Nessen, Paul. "Law Reporting: Another Case for Deregulation." *Modern Law Review* 48, no. 4 (July 1985): 412-433.

927. Waddams, Stephen. "Nineteenth-Century Treatises on English Contract Law." In *Law Books in Action: Essays on the Anglo-American Legal Treatise* (Angela

Fernandez & Markus D. Dubber, eds.; Oxford: Hart Publishing, 2012), 127-144.

928. Waddams, Stephen. "The Authority of Treatises in English Law (1800-1936)." In *Law and Authority in British Legal History, 1200-1900* (Mark Godfrey, ed.; Cambridge, UK: Cambridge University Press, 2016) 274-292.

929. Wagner, Frank D. "The Role of the Supreme Court Reporter in History." *Journal of Supreme Court History* 26, no. 1 (Mar. 2001): 9-24.

930. Wallach, Kate. "The Publication of Legal Treatises in America from 1800 to 1830." *Law Library Journal* 45, no. 3 (Aug. 1952): 136-147.

931. Wallach, Kate. *Bibliographical History of Louisiana Civil Law Sources: Roman, French and Spanish, With an Added Section on Modern French Research Materials.* Baton Rouge: Louisiana State Law Institute, 1955.

932. Wallinga, Tammo. "The Continuing Story of the Date and Origin of the Codex Florentinus." *Subseciva Groningana: Studies in Roman and Byzantine Law* 5 (1992), 7-20.

933. Wallinga, Tammo. "Authenticum and Authenticae - What's in a Name? References to Justinian's Novels in Medieval Manuscripts." *Tijdschrift voor Rechtsgeschiedenis / Legal History Review* 77, nos. 1-2 (Jan. 2009): 43-60.

934. Wallinga, Tammo. "The Common History of European Legal Scholarship." *Erasmus Law Review* 4, no. 1 (2011): 3-20. https://doi.org/10.5553/ELR221026712011004001002

935. Waterman, Julian S. "Thomas Jefferson and Blackstone's Commentaries." *Illinois Law Review* 27, no. 6 (1932-1933): 629-659.

936. Waters, Willard O. *Check List of American Laws, Charters and Constitutions of the 17th and 18th Centuries in*

the Huntington Library. San Marino, CA: Henry E. Huntington Library and Art Gallery, 1936.

937. Watson, Alan. "Justinian's Institutes and Some English Counterparts." In *Studies in Justinian's Institutes in Memory of J. A. C. Thomas* (Peter G. Stein & A. D. E. Lewis, eds.; London: Sweet & Maxwell, 1983), 164-180.

938. Watson, Alan. "The Structure of Blackstone's *Commentaries.*" *Yale Law Journal* 97, no. 5 (Apr. 1988): 795-822.

939. Watson, Alan. "Some Notes on Mackenzie's *Institutions* and the European Legal Tradition." *Ius Commune* 16 (1989): 303-313.

940. Watson, Alan. "The Importance of 'Nutshells'." *American Journal of Comparative Law* 42, no. 1 (Winter 1994): 1-23.

941. Wei, John C. "The Later Development of Gratian's *Decretum.*" In *Proceedings of the Fourteenth International Congress of Medieval Canon Law: Toronto, 5-11 August 2012* (Joseph Goering, Stephen Dusil & Andreas Thier, eds.; Città del Vaticano: Biblioteca Apostolica Vaticana, 2016), 149-159.

942. Werner, Wouter. "Prefaces and Authorship in International Law: The Example of Vitoria's *De Indis.*" *Law Text Culture* 23 (2019), 58-78. https://ro.uow.edu.au/ltc/vol23/iss1/5

943. Whisner, Mary. "That Most Congenial Lawyer/Bibliographer." *Law Library Journal* 104, no. 1 (Winter 2012): 135-147.

944. Whitman, James Q. "A Note on the Medieval Division of the Digest." *Tijdschrift voor Rechtsgeschiedenis / Legal History Review* 59, nos. 3-4 (Jan. 1991): 269-284.

945. Widener, Emma Molina, & Michael Widener. *Murder and Women in 19th-Century America: Trial Accounts in the Yale Law Library.* New Haven, CT: Lillian Goldman Law Library, Yale Law School, 2015.

946. Widener, Michael. "The Jamail Rastell Dictionary and Its Hidden Surprises." In *Language and the Law: Proceedings of a Conference, December 6-8, 2001, Tarlton Law Library, The University of Texas at Austin* (Marlyn Robinson, ed.; Buffalo, N.Y.: William S. Hein & Co., 2003), 3-13.

947. Widener, Michael. "Morris Cohen and the Art of Book Collecting." *Law Library Journal* 104, no. 1 (Winter 2012): 39-43.

948. Widener, Michael, & Mark S. Weiner. *Law's Picture Books: The Yale Law Library Collection.* Clark, NJ: Talbot Publishing, 2017.

949. Widener, Michael. "The Civil Law Collection of the Texas Supreme Court." *Journal of the Texas Supreme Court Historical Society* 8, no. 4 (Summer 2019): 17-39. https://texascourthistory.org/Content/Newsletters//TSCHS%20Summer%20Journal%202019rev.pdf

950. Widener, Michael. "From Law Book to Legal Book: The Origin of a Species." *Rechtsgeschichte - Legal History (Rg)* 29 (2021): 431-444.

951. Wiegand, Rudolf. "The Transmontane Decretists." In *The History of Medieval Canon Law in the Classical Period, 1140-1234: From Gratian to the Decretals of Gregory IX* (Wilfried Hartmann & Kenneth Pennington, eds.; Washington, DC: Catholic University of America Press, 2008), 174-210.

952. Wijffels, Alain A. *Late Sixteenth-Century Lists of Law Books at Merton College.* Cambridge, UK: LP Publications, 1992.

953. Wijffels, Alain A. "Law Books at Cambridge, 1500-1640." In *The Life of the Law: Proceedings of the Tenth British Legal History Conference, Oxford 1991* (Peter Birks, ed.; London: Hambledon Press, 1993), 59-87.

954. Wijffels, Alain A. "Law Books in Cambridge Libraries, 1500-1640." *Transactions of the Cambridge Bibliographical Society* 10, no. 3 (1993): 359-412.

955. Wijffels, Alain A. "Early-Modern Literature on International Law and the *Usus Modernus*." *Grotiana* 16-17, no. 1 (Jan. 1995): 35-54.

956. Wijffels, Alain A. "The Civil Law." In *The Cambridge History of the Book in Britain, Volume III, 1400-1557*, (Lotte Hellinga & J. B. Trapp, eds.; Cambridge: Cambridge University Press, 1999), 399-410.

957. Wijffels, Alain A. "From *Ius Commune* to Common Law, and Back Again: Legal Books at Trinity Hall: An Historical Perspective from the Old Library." In *Trinity Hall 2000. Legal Education and Learning. Proceedings of the Second Conference Held in July 1997 to Commemorate 650 Years of Education and Learning at Trinity Hall 1350-2000* (Alain A. Wijffels, ed.; Cambridge: Cambridge University Press, 1999), 33-42.

958. Wijffels, Alain A. "Tampering with the Code Civil 1804-2004." *Tijdschrift voor Rechtsgeschiedenis / Legal History Review* 72, nos. 3-4 (Jan. 2004): 195-214.

959. Wijffels, Alain A. "The Code de Procédure Civile (1806) in France, Belgium and the Netherlands." In *The French Code of Civil Procedure (1806) after 200 Years: The Civil Procedure Tradition in France and Abroad* (C. H. van Rhee, D. Heirbaut, & M. Storme, eds.; Mechelen: Kluwer, 2008), 5-73.

960. Wijffels, Alain A. "Legal Books and Legal Practice." In *The Old Library of the Supreme Court of the Netherlands* (J. G. B. Pikkemaat, ed.; Hilversum: Verloren, 2008), 21-38.

961. Wijffels, Alain A. "Early-Modern Scholarship on International Law." In *Research Handbook on the Theory and History of International Law* (A. Orakhelashvili, ed.; Cheltenham, UK & Northampton, MA: Edward Elgar 2011), 23-60.

962. Wijffels, Alain A. Book Review. *Tijdschrift voor Rechtsgeschiedenis / Legal History Review* 80, nos. 1-2 (Jan. 2012): 229-237. [Review essay of no. 695: Douglas J. Osler, *Jurisprudence of the Baroque: A Census of Seventeenth Century Italian Legal Imprints* (3 vols.; Frankfurt am Main: Vittorio Klostermann, 2009).]

963. Wijffels, Alain A. "Early-Modern *consilia* and *decisiones* in the Low Countries: The Lost Legacy of the *mos italicus*." In *Honos alit artes: studi per il settantesimo compleanno di Mario Ascheri* (4 vols.; Paola Maffei & Gian Maria Varanini, eds.; Firenze: Firenze University Press, 2014), 1:127-139.

964. Wijffels, Alain A. "Law Reports as Legal Authorities in Early Modern Belgian Legal Practice." In *Authorities in Early Modern Law Courts* (Guido Rossi, ed.; Edinburgh: Edinburgh University Press, 2021), 222-244.

965. Wilf, Steven. "Legal Treatise." In *The Oxford Handbook of Law and Humanities* (Simon Stern *et al.*, eds.; New York: Oxford University Press, 2020), 687-702.

966. Wilkie, Everett C. *The 1861 Texas Printings of the Ordinance of Secession, A Declaration of the Causes, and An Address to the People of Texas: An Illustrated Descriptive Printing History Commemorating the Sesquicentennial Anniversary of Their Adoption and the Secession of Texas from the United States of America.* Dallas: The Book Club of Texas, 2011.

967. Williams, Ian. "'He Creditted More the Printed Booke': Common Lawyers' Receptivity to Print, c. 1550-1640." *Law and History Review* 28, no. 1 (Feb. 2010): 39-70.

968. Williams, Ian. "A Medieval Book and Early-Modern Law: *Bracton*'s Authority and Application in the Common Law c. 1550-1640." *Tijdschrift voor Rechtsgeschiedenis / Legal History Review* 79, no. 1 (Jan. 2011): 47-80.

969. Williams, Ian. "The Tudor Genesis of Edward Coke's Immemorial Common Law." *The Sixteenth Century Journal* 43, no. 1 (Spring 2012): 103-123.

970. Williams, Ian. "Common Law Scholarship and the Written Word." In *The Oxford Handbook of English Law and Literature, 1500-1700* (Lorna Hutson, ed.; Oxford; New York: Oxford University Press, 2017), 61-79.

971. Williams, Ian. "Changes to Common Law Printing in the 1630s: Unlawful, Unreliable, Dishonest." *Journal of Legal History* 39, no. 3 (Dec. 2018): 225-252.

972. Williams, Ian. "Law, Language and the Printing Press in the Reign of Charles I: Explaining the Printing of the Common Law in English." *Law and History Review* 38, no. 2 (May 2020): 339-371.

973. Wilson, Adelyn L. M. "Stair and the *Inleydinge* of Grotius." *Edinburgh Law Review* 14, no. 2 (May 2010): 259-268.

974. Winfield, Percy H. "Abridgments of the Year Books." *Harvard Law Review* 37, no. 2 (Dec. 1923): 214-244.

975. Winfield, Percy H. "Early Attempts at Reporting Cases." *Law Quarterly Review* 40, no. 3 (1924): 316-323.

976. Winfield, Percy H. *The Chief Sources of English Legal History*. Cambridge, MA: Harvard University Press, 1925.

977. Winroth, Anders. *The Making of Gratian's Decretum.* New York: Cambridge University Press, 2000.

978. Winroth, Anders, & Michael Widener. *The Pope's Other Jobs: Judge and Lawgiver*. New Haven: Lillian Goldman Law Library, Yale Law School, 2015.

979. Winroth, Anders. "Gratian and His Book: How a Medieval Teacher Changed European Law and Religion." *Oxford Journal of Law and Religion* 10, no. 1 (Feb. 2021): 1-15.

980. Winroth, Anders. "Hólar and Belgsdalsbók." *Gripla* 32 (2021): 151-164. https://doi.org/10.33112/gripla.32.6

981. Winston, Jessica. "Legal Satire and the Legal Profession in the 1590s: John Davies's Epigrammes and Professional Decorum." In *The Oxford Handbook of English Law and*

Literature, 1500-1700 (Lorna Hutson, ed.; Oxford; New York: Oxford University Press, 2017), 121-142.

982. Wolf, Edwin, II. "The Library of a Philadelphia Judge, 1708." *Pennsylvania Magazine of History & Biography* 83, no. 2 (Apr. 1959): 180-191.

983. Wolf, Edwin, II. "The Library of Ralph Assheton: The Book Background of a Colonial Philadelphia Lawyer." *Papers of the Bibliographical Society of America* 58, no. 4 (Dec. 1964): 345-379.

984. Wolf, Edwin, II. "Lawyers and Law Books." In *The Book Culture of a Colonial American City: Philadelphia Books, Bookmen and Booksellers* (E. Wolf, ed.; Oxford: Clarendon Press, 1988), 131-163.

985. Woxland, Thomas A. "Forever Associated with the Practice of Law: The Early Years of the West Publishing Company." *Legal Reference Services Quarterly* 5, no. 1 (Spring 1985): 115-124.

986. Woxland, Thomas A., & Patti J. Ogden. *Landmarks in American Legal Publishing: An Exhibit Catalog.* St. Paul, MN: West, 1989.

987. Wright, Barry. "Renovate or Rebuild? Treatises, Digests and Criminal Law Codification." In *Law Books in Action: Essays on the Anglo-American Legal Treatise* (Angela Fernandez & Markus D. Dubber, eds.; Oxford: Hart Publishing, 2012), 181-201.

988. Wright, Nancy E. "John Cowell and *The Interpreter*: Law, Authority, and Attribution in Seventeenth-Century England." *Australian Journal of Legal History* 1, no. 1 (1995): 11-36.

989. Yale, D. E. C. "St. German's Little Treatise Concerning Writs of Subpoena." *Irish Jurist* 10, no. 2 (1975): 324-333.

990. Yale, D. E. C. "'Of No Mean Authority': Some Later Uses of Bracton." In *On the Laws and Customs of England: Essays in Honor of Samuel E. Thorne* (Morris

S. Arnold *et al.*, eds.; Chapel Hill: University of North Carolina Press, 1981), 383-396.

991. Yarger, Susan Rice. *State Constitutional Conventions, 1959-1975: A Bibliography.* Westport, CT: Greenwood Press, 1976.

992. Yates, Sarah. "Black's Law Dictionary: The Making of an American Standard." *Law Library Journal* 103, no. 2 (Spring 2011): 175-198.

993. Yiannopoulos, A. N. "The Early Sources of Louisiana Law: Critical Appraisal of a Controversy." In *Louisiana's Legal Heritage* (Edward E Haas, ed.; Pensacola, FL: Perdido Bay Press for the Louisiana State Museum, 1983), 87-106.

994. Young, Thomas J., Jr. "A Look at American Law Reporting in the 19th Century." *Law Library Journal* 68, no. 3 (Aug. 1975): 294-306.

995. Zhang, Ting. *Circulating the Code: Print Media and Legal Knowledge in Qing China.* Seattle: University of Washington Press, 2020.

996. Zimmermann, Reinhard. "Law Journals in Nineteenth-Century Scotland." *Edinburgh Law Review* 12, no. 1 (Jan. 2008): 9-25.

997. Zwalve, W. J., & Th. de Vries. "The New Temple: On the Origin, Nature and Composition of the *partes Digestorum.*" *Tijdschrift voor Rechtsgeschiedenis / Legal History Review* 85, nos. 3-4 (Dec. 2017): 492-521.

998. Zwalve, W. J., & Th. de Vries. "The Navel: Reflections on the Composition of the *Quinta pars Digestorum.*" *Tijdschrift voor Rechtsgeschiedenis / Legal History Review* 88, nos. 3-4 (Dec. 2020): 591-604.

Index of Co-authors

Appendices

Appendix 1

Leading Journals (6 or more articles)

Journal title	No. of articles cited
Law Library Journal	95
American Journal of Legal History	22
Legal Reference Services Quarterly	17
Grotiana	16
Journal of Legal History	16
Irish Jurist	12
Unbound: An Annual Review of Legal History and Rare Books	12
Tijdschrift voor Rechtsgeschiedenis / Legal History Review	11
Law Quarterly Review	10
Jus Gentium: Journal of International Legal History	9
Cambridge Law Journal	7
Rechtsgeschichte - Legal History (Rg)	7
The Library: Transactions of the Bibliographical Society	7
Ius Commune	6
The Green Bag, 2nd ser.	6

Appendix 2

Leading Collective Works (6 or more chapters)

	No. of citations	Item nos.
Law Books in Action: Essays on the Anglo-American Legal Treatise (Oxford: Hart Publishing, 2012).	11	16, 170, 295, 315, 321, 371, 467, 715, 732, 927, 987
Learning the Law: Teaching and the Transmission of Law in England, 1150-1900 (London: Hambledon Press, 1999).	10	65, 116, 229, 617, 640, 730, 731, 744, 822, 847
"Esteemed bookes of lawe" and the Legal Culture of Early Virginia (Charlottesville: University of Virginia Press, 2017).	9	84, 89, 133, 147, 409, 416, 426, 896, 904
Collecting and Managing Rare Law Books: Papers Presented at a Conference Celebrating the Dedication of the New Tarlton Law Library (Dobbs Ferry, NY: Oceana Publications, 1981).	8	14, 207, 353, 737, 738, 776, 901, 911
Re-interpreting Blackstone's Commentaries: A Seminal Text in National and International Contexts (Oxford, UK: Hart Publishing, 2014).	8	164, 569, 598, 627, 650, 676, 747, 839
Reassessing Legal Humanism and Its Claims: Petere Fontes? (Edinburgh: Edinburgh University Press, 2016).	8	54, 417, 478, 489, 586, 697, 880, 917
Authorities in Early Modern Law Courts (Edinburgh: Edinburgh University Press, 2021).	7	176, 364, 480, 583, 637, 733, 964

The History of Medieval Canon Law in the Classical Period, 1140-1234: From Gratian to the Decretals of Gregory IX (Washington, DC: Catholic University of America Press, 2008).	7	298, 444, 549, 725, 726, 727, 951
Case Law in the Making: The Techniques and Methods of Judicial Records and Law Reports (Berlin: Duncker & Humblot, 1997).	6	28, 143, 144, 412, 474, 475
Law Reporting in Britain (London: Hambledon Press, 1995).	6	27, 114, 142, 189, 471, 588
The Cambridge History of the Book in Britain, Vols. 3-5 (Cambridge: Cambridge University Press, 1999).	6	30, 31, 413, 743, 768, 956
The Power of the Book: Medial Approaches to Medieval Nordic Legal Manuscripts (Berlin: Nordeuropa-Institut der Humboldt-Universität, 2014).	6	8, 107, 127, 499, 503, 795

Entire Volumes:

168. *The Cambridge History of Medieval Canon Law* (Cambridge, UK: Cambridge University Press, 2022).

347. *The Formation and Transmission of Western Legal Culture: 150 Books That Made the Law in the Age of Printing* (Cham, Switzerland: Springer, 2016).

482. *An Introductory Survey of the Sources and Literature of Scots Laws* (Edinburgh: Printed for the Stair Society by R. Maclehose & Co., 1936).

553. *Law and the Christian Tradition in Italy: The Legacy of the Great Jurists* (New York: Routledge, 2021).

741. *Pre-Statehood Legal Materials: A Fifty-state Research Guide, Including the District of Columbia and New York City* (2 vols.; Binghamton, NY: Haworth Press, 2006).

860. *Stair Tercentenary Studies* (Edinburgh: The Stair Society, 1981).

924. *Virginia Law Books: Essays and Bibliographies* (Philadelphia: American Philosophical Society, 2000).

Appendix 3

Index of Leading Authors (6 or more titles)

Author (no. of titles)	Item nos.
Hoeflich, Michael H. (30)	177, 427-453, 624, 751
Baker, John H. (23)	19-41
Osler, Douglas J. (20)	318, 680-698
Cohen, Morris L. (15)	192-205, 661
Wijffels, Alain A. (15)	176, 474, 952-964
Bryson, William Hamilton (13)	137-149
Fishman, Joel (13)	331-343
Davis, Laurel (12)	82, 255-265
Ibbetson, David J. (10)	471-480
Somos, Mark (10)	220-228, 857
Widener, Michael (10)	15, 599, 748, 945-950, 978
Billings, Warren M. (9)	84-92
Corredera, Edward Jones (9)	220-228
Brand, Paul (8)	112-119
Cairns, John W. (8)	159-166
Dolezalek, Gero R. (8)	277-284
Parise, Agustín (8)	394, 707-713
Lind, Douglas W. (7)	560-566
Pennington, Kenneth (7)	723-729
Prest, Wilfrid (7)	742-748
Stein, Peter (7)	864-870
Bilder, Mary Sarah (6)	62, 81-82, 263-264, 666
Butler, William E (6).	152-156, 448
Musson, Anthony (6)	654-659
Surrency, Erwin C. (6)	885-890
Williams, Ian (6)	967-972

Appendix 4

Summary of index headings

Subject type	Works refer- enced	Refer- ences	Head- ings
Bodies of law	881	1,473	179
Legal genres	464	573	79
Bibliographic topics	409	523	58
Names	263	312	149
Bibliographic genres	184	238	43
Chronological periods	165	189	17
Legal topics	60	65	16

About the Authors

Michael Widener was the Rare Book Librarian in the Lillian Goldman Law Library, Yale Law School, from 2006 until his retirement in April 2021. Prior to that he was Head of Special Collections in the Tarlton Law Library, University of Texas at Austin, from 1991 to 2006. Since 2010 he has served on the faculty of the Rare Book School, University of Virginia, teaching the course "Law Books: History & Connoisseurship." He has presented papers on rare books and archives to conferences in the U.S., Australia, Brazil, Italy, Mexico, and Sweden, including the 2017 Rare Book Lecture at the University of Melbourne. He is co-author (with Mark S. Weiner) of *Law's Picture Books: The Yale Law Library Collection* (Talbot Publishing, 2017), the catalogue of a major exhibition at the Grolier Club, which won the 2018 Joseph L. Andrews Legal Literature Award from the American Association of Law Libraries. He holds a master's degree in library and information science from The University of Texas at Austin.

Ryan Greenwood earned a B.A. from the University of Chicago, M.A. and Ph.D. from the University of Toronto, and a M.L.I.S. from Rutgers University. He has been Curator of Rare Books and Special Collections at the University of Minnesota Law Library since 2014. He has served on the faculty of Rare Book School, University of Virginia, assisting Michael Widener in the course, "Law Books: History & Connoisseurship." In 2013-14, he was the Rare Book Fellow at the Lillian Goldman Law Library, Yale Law School. Greenwood is co-author, with Patrick Graybill, of the special collections catalog, *Jewels of the Collection: Treasures of the Riesenfeld Rare Books Research Center*, which won the 2024 Joseph L. Andrews Legal Literature Award from the American Association of Law Libraries. He has taught and published on legal history and special collections.

S et in Times New Roman. The typeface was commissioned by the British newspaper *The Times* in 1931 and conceived by Stanley Morison, the artistic adviser to the British branch of the printing equipment company Monotype, in collaboration with Victor Lardent, a lettering artist in The Times's advertising department. The typeface is based on Plantin.

Interior design and composition
by Brian H W Hill
Cover design
by Peter Lo Ricco

www.ingramcontent.com/pod-product-compliance
Lightning Source LLC
Chambersburg PA
CBHW021500180326
41458CB00051B/6897/J